LY HAM

DEBATING EUTHANASIA

In this new addition to the Debating Law series, Emily Jackson and John Keown re-examine the legal and ethical aspects of the euthanasia debate.

Emily Jackson argues that we owe it to everyone in society to do all that we can to ensure that they experience a 'good death'. For a small minority of patients who experience intolerable and unrelievable suffering, this may mean helping them to have an assisted death. In a liberal society, where people's moral views differ, we should not force individuals to experience deaths they find intolerable. This is not an argument in favour of dying. On the contrary, Jackson argues that legalisation could extend and enhance the lives of people whose present fear of the dying process causes them overwhelming distress.

John Keown argues that voluntary euthanasia and physician-assisted suicide are gravely unethical, and he defends their continued prohibition by law. He analyses the main arguments for relaxation of the law – including those which invoke the experience of jurisdictions which permit these practices – and finds them wanting. Relaxing the law would, he concludes, be both wrong in principle and dangerous in practice, not least for the dying, the disabled and the disadvantaged.

Volume 3 in the series Debating Law

Debating Law

General Editor: Professor Peter Cane, the Australian National University

Debating Law is a new, exciting series edited by Peter Cane that gives scholarly experts the opportunity to offer contrasting perspectives on significant topics of contemporary, general interest.

Debating Euthanasia

Emily Jackson
and
John Keown

·H A R T·
PUBLISHING

OXFORD AND PORTLAND, OREGON
2012

Published in the United Kingdom by Hart Publishing Ltd
16C Worcester Place, Oxford, OX1 2JW
Telephone: +44 (0)1865 517530
Fax: +44 (0)1865 510710
E-mail: mail@hartpub.co.uk
Website: http://www.hartpub.co.uk

Published in North America (US and Canada) by
Hart Publishing
c/o International Specialized Book Services
920 NE 58th Avenue, Suite 300
Portland, OR 97213-3786
USA
Tel: +1 503 287 3093 or toll-free: (1) 800 944 6190
Fax: +1 503 280 8832
E-mail: orders@isbs.com
Website: http://www.isbs.com

British Library Cataloguing in Publication Data
Data Available

ISBN: 978-1-84946-178-8

Typeset by Hope Services, Abingdon
Printed and bound in Great Britain by
Page Bros Ltd, Norwich, Norfolk

Series Editor's Preface

This innovative and exciting series was inspired by one of the best-known philosophy books of the latter half of the twentieth century. *Utilitarianism for and against* by JJC Smart and Bernard Williams, published in 1973, is described on its cover as '[t]wo essays . . . written from opposite points of view'. It is one of the classics of the modern literature on utilitarianism. Based on this model, books in the *Debating Law* series will contain two essays of around 30,000 words, each developing a strong and intellectually rigorous argument on a topic of contemporary and ongoing debate. The aim is to stimulate, challenge and inform by bringing contrasting perspectives together in the one volume.

The *Debating Law* series offers a forum for scholarly argument and advocacy. It gives essayists the opportunity to make a fresh and provocative statement of a normative position freed from a tight requirement of 'balance'. Although debaters are encouraged to exchange ideas during the writing process, it is not the intention that the two essays will answer one another but rather that each will provide an independent statement of a point of view. Authors may take different tacks and address different issues within the broad topic, and the starting points or foundations of the case on one side may be different from those of the case on the other side. The confident expectation is that the debate format will sharpen issues, and highlight areas of both agreement and disagreement, in an effective and illuminating way.

The *Debating Law* series is designed for a wide readership. The aim is that each essay should be self-contained, accessibly written and only lightly end-noted. Books in the series will be valuable for those coming to the topic for the first time and also for the experienced reader seeking a stimulating, thought-provoking and concise statement of different points of view. They will provide valuable resources for teaching as well as lively discussions of important issues of wide current interest.

Peter Cane

Acknowledgements — John Keown

I am grateful to Professors John Finnis, Luke Gormally, Christopher Kaczor and Damien Keown, who read and commented on all or part of my contribution to this volume. I remain solely responsible for my contribution's accuracy and argument.

I dedicate my contribution to this book to Alfonso Gómez-Lobo, the Ryan Professor of Metaphysics and Moral Philosophy at Georgetown University, and to Dr Amanda Perreau-Saussine, Fellow of Queens' College, Cambridge.

Acknowledgements – Emily Jackson

I am very grateful to Hugh Collins, Daniel Slater, Robert Phillips and Clive Seale for their comments on an earlier version of my contribution, and to Peter Cane for his invaluable editorial suggestions. I benefited enormously from attending a workshop on prospective legal immunity at Kings College, London, organised by Roger Brownsword, Penney Lewis and Genevra Richardson, so my thanks are also due to them, and to the other participants at that event.

Contents

In Favour of the Legalisation of Assisted Dying

Emily Jackson

———✦———

I. INTRODUCTION

THE CORE of my argument is that we owe it to people who experience permanent and irreversible suffering, and to those who justifiably worry that this lies ahead of them, to do all that we can to alleviate their distress. In a very small number of cases, this may entail allowing people who cannot be helped in any other way, and who believe that death offers the only possible release from their suffering, to have their lives ended quickly and painlessly.

This might be through *euthanasia*: which derives from the Greek *eu* (good) and *thanatos* (death), but which has acquired a more specific modern usage. The *Oxford English Dictionary*'s definition is 'a gentle and easy death, the bringing about of this, especially in the case of incurable and painful disease'. While the *OED* does not specify exactly how the gentle and easy death is to be brought about, it is generally assumed that euthanasia refers to a third party deliberating ending a person's life. Legalised euthanasia would normally involve a doctor giving a patient a lethal injection. If instead a close relative were to end a person's life in order to relieve their suffering, that would not generally be described as euthanasia, rather it might be a case of *mercy killing*.

Euthanasia is sometimes referred to more specifically as voluntary active euthanasia (VAE), in order to distinguish it from *involuntary* and *passive* euthanasia. In *involuntary euthanasia*, a person's life would be ended without their request: an example might be giving a lethal injection to someone who is permanently comatose. Causing death through the withdrawal of life-prolonging medical treatment is sometimes described as *passive euthanasia*, but since 'treatment withdrawal' is a less value-laden term, I shall simply refer to treatment withdrawal and I will not use the term passive euthanasia.

In *assisted suicide*, the person who dies ends their own life, but they are helped to do so by a third party. Legalised assisted suicide would be likely to involve a doctor helping a patient to die by prescribing a lethal dose of medication, which the patient then takes him or herself; this is sometimes described more specifically as physician assisted suicide (PAS). The person assisting the suicide need not be a doctor, however, and so I shall simply refer to assisted suicide, rather than PAS.

Later in this essay, I discuss the relative merits of legalising euthanasia and/or assisted suicide. Each has advantages and disadvantages, but the question of which method should be preferred is secondary to the central question of whether it is sometimes acceptable to deliberately do something to help bring about a patient's death. As a result, I will also use the term *assisted dying* to refer to both euthanasia and assisted suicide.

So why might someone ask for an assisted death? In 2009 Robert Baxter, a 75-year-old retired truck driver who had been suffering from lymphocytic leukaemia, posthumously won his claim against the State of Montana that he had a right to die 'with dignity'. According to the Montana Supreme Court, this should have extended to offering protection from liability under the State's homicide laws to a physician who prescribed him lethal medication.[1] After his death, his daughter told the Court that he

---

[1]   *Baxter v Montana* 224 P 3d 1211 (Mont Sup Ct 2009).

had 'yearned for death', and in his affidavit he had set out clearly and eloquently why he thought he should have the right to 'aid in dying':

> As a result of the leukaemia and the treatment I have received to combat it, I have suffered varying symptoms including anaemia, chronic fatigue and weakness, nausea, night sweats, intermittent and persistent infections, massively swollen glands, easy bruising, significant ongoing digestive problems and generalized pain and discomfort. These symptoms, as well as others, are expected to increase in frequency and intensity as the chemotherapy loses its effectiveness and the disease progresses.
>
> Given the nature of my illness, I have no reasonable prospect of cure or recovery. As the cancer takes its toll, I face the progressive erosion of bodily function and integrity, increasing pain and suffering, and the loss of my personal dignity.
>
> I have lived a good and a long life, and have no wish to leave this world prematurely. As death approaches from my disease, however, if my suffering becomes unbearable I want the legal option of being able to die in a peaceful and dignified manner by consuming medication prescribed by my doctor for that purpose. Because it will be my suffering, my life, and my death that will be involved, I seek the right and responsibility to make that critical choice for myself if circumstances lead me to do so. I feel strongly that this intensely personal and private decision should be left to me and my conscience – based on my most deeply held values and beliefs, after consulting with my family and doctor – and that the government should not have the right to prohibit this choice by criminalizing the aid in dying procedure.[2]

Win Crew, whose husband Reg was one of the first UK citizens to die in a Dignitas clinic in Switzerland, explained why he had chosen an assisted death:

> My husband suffered terribly as a result of MND [motor neurone disease]. Only weeks after the diagnosis he was unable to move his arms, depending on family and carers to feed him, wash him, dress him. This progressed to his legs, and in no time at all, he could neither feed himself nor go to the toilet, and he had to sleep and live in

---

[2] http://community.compassionandchoices.org/document.doc?id=20.

a chair. He was barely able to support his own head, and was told by doctors that he would soon have to be fed from a peg [a feeding tube].

As each day passed, Reg found his life increasingly unbearable – a living hell. Palliative care did little for him. His dignity was stripped away, each time the disease closed down another part of his body, and so was his independence. Reg loved life, but not in the incapacitated shell of his former self.[3]

Tony Nicklinson, a 54-year-old British man who has suffered from locked-in syndrome since having a stroke in 2006, has explained why he wants to be helped to die:

I need help in almost every aspect of my life. I cannot scratch if I itch, I cannot pick my nose if it is blocked and I can only eat if I am fed like a baby – only I won't grow out of it, unlike the baby. I have no privacy or dignity left. I am washed, dressed and put to bed by carers who are, after all, still strangers. I am fed up with my life and don't want to spend the next 20 years or so like this. Am I grateful that the Athens doctors saved my life? No, I am not. If I had my time again, and knew then what I know now, I would not have called the ambulance but let nature take its course.[4]

My claim in this essay will be that, in the absence of evidence that an effective assisted dying law is actually *infeasible*, we should not abandon patients like Robert Baxter, Reg Crew and Tony Nicklinson. This is not an argument in favour of death. On the contrary, I will argue that a regulated system in which euthanasia and/or assisted suicide was an option could extend and enhance the lives of people facing the prospect of a prolonged and distressing decline. A recent study of patients suffering from advanced cancer found that the option of assisted death operated as a 'hypothetical exit plan', which provided reassurance and enhanced their ability to tolerate the present burdens of

---

[3] Personal story, www.dignityindying.org.uk/personal-stories.
[4] Robert Booth, '"Locked-in" syndrome man demands right to die' *The Guardian* (19 July 2010).

treatment.[5] The prospect of being able to maintain control and autonomy at the end of life is therefore of value to many more patients than would ever actually opt for an assisted death.

It is also important to note at the outset that there is a critical difference between my position and that of opponents of assisted dying. Supporters of assisted dying recognise that not everyone shares the view that it is acceptable. I would vigorously support and uphold the right of every person to reject assisted dying for themselves, and the right of every healthcare professional to con-scientiously object to playing any part at all in its provision. Both access to and participation in assisted dying must be optional and voluntary, and the personal beliefs of those who would want nothing to do with it must be respected. In contrast, opponents of assisted dying do seek to impose their belief that it is wrong on others whose views are different. In a secular society, where we recognise that our fundamental moral values differ, shouldn't we respect both the beliefs of people like Tony Nicklinson, who feel strongly that they should have access to assisted dying *and* the beliefs of opponents of assisted dying, who would reject it for themselves?

It is also important to recognise that people like Robert Baxter, Reg Crew and Tony Nicklinson do not seek death lightly. Of course, a request for assisted death should prompt us to investigate other ways to alleviate the person's suffering, before steps are taken to end their life. But if someone asks for an assisted death, it would be patronising and heartless to presuppose that their desire for death is just a passing response to temporary discomfort. Decisions about how we die are – as six distinguished American philosophers explained in their joint submission to the US Supreme Court in 1997 – significant and deeply personal issues of conscience:

> Certain decisions are momentous in their impact on the character of a person's life – decisions about religious faith, political and moral

---

[5] R Nissim, L Gagliese and G Rodin, 'The Desire for Hastened Death in Individuals with Advanced Cancer: A Longitudinal Qualitative Study' (2009) 69 *Social Science & Medicine* 165–71.

allegiance, marriage, procreation, and death, for example. Such deeply personal decisions pose controversial questions about how and why human life has value. In a free society, individuals must be allowed to make those decisions for themselves, out of their own faith, conscience, and convictions . . . Most of us see death – whatever we think will follow it – as the final act of life's drama, and we want that last act to reflect our own convictions, those we have tried to live by, not the convictions of others forced on us in our most vulnerable moment.[6]

My argument will proceed as follows. First, I will explain in more detail why I believe that we should try to design a law which permits assisted dying in certain limited circumstances. Next, I will consider a range of counter-arguments which my opponents might invoke in order to establish that legalisation would be either wrong ('in principle' objections), or dangerous ('regulatory difficulty' objections).

Those with faith-based objections to assisted dying commonly cite additional secular arguments against legalisation; but if someone believes assisted dying is morally wrong, proving that regulatory objections are not insurmountable will, in practice, make no difference to them. Where the 'in principle' objection to assisted dying is grounded in a person's religious belief, there is almost certainly nothing I or anyone else could do to persuade them that assisted dying is sometimes an acceptable response to unbearable suffering. But it is important to remember that I am not asking someone with a religious objection to assisted dying to change his or her mind. On the contrary, my claim is that people who object to a practice on faith grounds ought to recognise that the law should not insist that others, who do not share their faith, must have their freedom restricted in order to satisfy a religious tenet which makes no sense to them.

There are people who have faith-based objections to homosexuality. Of course, this means that they are free not to engage in

---

[6] Ronald Dworkin, Thomas Nagel, Robert Nozick, John Rawls, Thomas Scanlon and Judith Jarvis Thomson presented an Amici Curiae Brief for Respondents – referred to as The Philosophers' Brief – to the Supreme Court in two cases heard at the same time (*Washington et al v Glucksberg* 117 S Ct 2258 (1997) and *Vacco v Quill* 117 S Ct 2293 (1997)).

homosexual behaviour themselves: the legalisation of homosexual sex did not make it compulsory. But it does not give them the right to tell others, who do not share their beliefs, how to live their lives. We are entitled to make choices about our own conduct according to our own religious values, but we are not – in a liberal, secular democracy – entitled to foist those values on others.

In contrast to 'in principle' arguments against legalisation, secular regulatory objections to assisted dying are often essentially empirical claims that legalising assisted dying would have a range of undesirable consequences. Relevant here, of course, is the fact that some variation of assisted dying is lawful in a number of jurisdictions: namely the Netherlands, Belgium, Switzerland and Luxembourg, in Europe, and the states of Oregon and Washington in the US. Evidence from these places is clearly relevant and useful when considering regulatory objections to assisted dying and whether they can be effectively overcome, but multiple factors may affect our ability to 'read across' from one country's experience to the likely effects of legalisation in another. For example, the Dutch have very high levels of trust in the medical profession in general, and in their family doctors in particular. In Belgium, there is an exceptionally well funded system of palliative care. As a result, claiming that the Dutch system would function well in a country where doctors are not trusted as much, or that the Belgian system would work when funding for palliative care is patchy, might be problematic.

I am not going to pretend that all of the arguments against assisted dying are groundless. Clearly, since the result will be a person's death, there are reasons for taking very seriously objections to legalisation, based upon the possibility that we might mistakenly believe someone's request was voluntary, or that they were competent, or indeed that they were in fact terminally ill. My point will instead be that none of the various objections to legalisation is sufficiently compelling to justify a refusal even to attempt to devise an effective assisted dying law.

Finally, it might be thought that this modest argument – that we should at least try to design an effective assisted dying law –

does not take us very far. But at the end of this essay I will reiterate that a refusal to contemplate legalisation of assisted dying has costs and negative consequences which – when placed in the balance with the challenges that arise from legalisation – should lead us to put as much effort as we can into alleviating the suffering which prompts patients' requests for assisted dying. I am certainly not suggesting that euthanasia should be the first response to such a request. On the contrary, there is often much that can be done to improve patients' quality of life, even when they believe their condition to be hopeless. But if we don't admit that there are some patients whose suffering cannot be relieved by palliative care or social support services, or even by love, we are disbelieving the accounts of people who know more about their own suffering than we ever could. We owe it to them to do all we can to provide the care and support that will help them avoid the 'loss of self' that commonly prompts requests for assisted dying, but when we cannot do any more, I will argue that we also owe it to them to honour and respect their desire for a peaceful death.

II. WHY WE SHOULD TRY

There is, most commonly among a subset of patients suffering from terminal conditions – such as cancer and motor neurone disease – a strong and understandable desire for more control over the dying process which they know lies ahead of them. In the West, most people now die from degenerative diseases, like cancer, which can result in a slow and drawn-out decline. As well as prolonging patients' lives, medicine has also prolonged and medicalised the experience of dying, with more and more of us experiencing protracted, institutional deaths. Life-prolonging technologies not only enable us to live longer, but are also responsible for 'the ever lengthening twilight that divides life from death.'[7]

Of course, all of us will die, and so the choice is not between an assisted death and not dying at all. Rather, and to put it bluntly,

---

[7] TW Furlow, 'Euthanasia and the Tyranny of Technology' in M Kohl (ed), *Beneficent Euthanasia* (New York, Buffalo Books, 1975).

the options are dying now or dying later. In choosing an assisted death, a patient is essentially opting for an earlier death, over which they are able to exercise some control, in preference to a later death, where control may be absent, and which may be preceded by a period of extreme dependency.

All of the available evidence suggests that what people fear most towards the end of life is seldom pain, but what I will refer to as 'loss of self'. Surveys from Oregon and the Netherlands consistently show that the principal motivations for seeking assisted death are loss of autonomy (in Oregon in 2009, this was cited by 96.6 per cent of people who sought access to assisted suicide); loss of dignity (91.5 per cent); decreasing ability to participate in activities that made life enjoyable (86.4 per cent) and losing control of bodily functions (52.5 per cent). Inadequate pain control, or concern about it, was much less commonly cited (10.2 per cent).[8]

In one study of the reasons for people's interest in assisted suicide, a patient with metastatic lung cancer explained what he meant by his fractured sense of dignity:

> And I was on the commode and I had to be wiped and I just about cried my eyes out because of . . . you know, I never felt . . . I said to the nurses, God, who would have ever thought it would ever come down to this. I got these diapers or whatever it is that they call it . . . And that's presenting a problem. I don't like to think of myself as that. Things like that. That's my dignity and it comes down to types of things like that really . . . So I get mad.[9]

And a study of people living with AIDS again found participants used the notion of 'dignity' to describe their experiences:

> You've become a bag of potatoes to be moved from spot to spot, to be rushed back and forth from the hospital, to be carried to your doctors' appointments or wheeled in a wheelchair, and it really

---

[8] Oregon Department of Human Services, *Twelfth Annual Report on Oregon's Death with Dignity Act* (2009) www.oregon.gov/DHS/ph/pas/docs/yr12-tbl-1.pdf.

[9] HM Chochinov, T Hack, T Hassard, LJ Kristjanson, S McClement and M Harlos, 'Dignity in the Terminally Ill: A Cross-Sectional, Cohort Study' (2002) 360 *The Lancet* 2026–30.

does take away any self-worth, any dignity, or any will to continue to live.[10]

The term 'human dignity' has a number of heavily contested meanings in the field of bioethics. It is, for example, often used in debates over what, if anything, marks humans out as having a special sort of 'dignity' which distinguishes them from other animals. But these patients are not invoking 'dignity' here as a measure of their special worth as human beings. Rather, these patients are using the word 'dignity' to capture the way in which their lack of independence interferes with their sense of self. It is not an externally attributed 'badge' of value in this context, but an internal sense of wanting their death, and the dying process which precedes it, to be consistent with the values that have been important to them during their life.

Opponents of assisted dying often suggest that high-quality palliative care is a better solution to the problems faced by these patients than helping them to die. This view is held especially strongly by experts in palliative medicine,[11] which should undoubtedly give us pause for thought. If people who spend their lives caring for the dying believe that, with optimum palliative care, no one need experience intolerable suffering at the end of life, should we not acknowledge their superior expertise, and think seriously about the claim that assisted death is, in some ways, a 'cop-out' from the expense and commitment of providing excellent palliative care to everyone who could benefit from it?

Perhaps; though I would maintain that the true 'expert' in relation to the existence, or otherwise, of unbearable suffering is the patient herself. There is now a wealth of empirical evidence concerning the motivations of patients who express an interest in assisted dying, and it is clear that they often believe that their life has ceased to be any sort of life *to them*. Importantly, requests for

[10] JV Lavery, J Boyle, BM Dickens, H Maclean and PA Singer, 'Origins of the Desire for Euthanasia and Assisted Suicide in People with HIV-1 or AIDS: A Qualitative Study' (2001) 358 *The Lancet* 362–67

[11] A Maaike, MA Hermsen, AMJ Henk and MD ten Have, 'Euthanasia in Palliative Care Journals' (2002) 23 *Journal of Pain and Symptom Management* 517–25.

assisted dying are generally not prompted only by a person's medical symptoms – pain, loss of mobility etc – but by the social or psychological consequences of those symptoms. Of course, it would be a mistake to think that there is a clear boundary between the two. Incontinence may be a physical symptom, but the prospect of spending the rest of one's life wearing nappies, or never again being able to go to the toilet on one's own, is not just inconvenient; it may also take its toll on one's psychological wellbeing. Palliative care specialists are undoubtedly well equipped now to manage pain, although it should be noted that some powerful analgesic drugs have unpleasant side-effects, and because some of them can be addictive, patients may find themselves experiencing withdrawal symptoms and the indignity of addiction. But even if inadequate pain management *should* be a thing of the past, it is much less clear that palliative care can alleviate the psychosocial consequences of bodily decline.

Some palliative care experts have argued that we should not take requests for assisted dying 'at face value', and should instead explore their 'covert meaning'.[12] While it may be true that the desire to die can be a temporary response to a feeling of overwhelming hopelessness, and that it would be crucial to explore whether this is the case before moving towards complying with a patient's request, this is an argument for a robust filter on access to assisted death, which should include psychological assessment and an exploration of alternative ways to alleviate the patient's distress. But to claim that assisted death could *never* be justifiable, and that a patient's request for an assisted death is always essentially just a 'cry for help', is to disbelieve patients' accounts of their own suffering. In addition to those whose initial anguish can be effectively addressed with high-quality care and social support, there will also be patients whose desire for death turns out – after further investigation – to be permanent and incurable.

Someone who is dying has often lost control over most aspects of their life. A patient who is in the final stages of terminal cancer

[12] YY Wood Mak and G Elwyn, 'Voices of the Terminally Ill: Uncovering the Meaning of Desire for Euthanasia' (2005) 19 *Palliative Medicine* 343–50.

will have a catheter to collect their urine. They may have a colostomy bag for their faeces, though more commonly they may simply have to wear dressings, a bit like diapers or nappies, which are changed regularly. They will be unable to feed or wash themselves and will have virtually no privacy. Some patients are stoical in the face of this loss of capacity for self-care, whereas others find it unbearable. If it is extreme dependency that prompts requests for assisted dying, it should not surprise us that in countries where euthanasia or assisted suicide has been legalised, requests tend to come from younger, more affluent people with terminal illnesses, who may experience the loss of autonomy especially keenly.

Interestingly too, there is evidence from Belgium of a higher incidence of euthanasia among patients who had received spiritual care in the last three months of life.[13] For these patients, being helped to come to terms with death was not an *alternative* to euthanasia. Indeed, in the UK there is evidence that people who have received good hospice and palliative care are *more* rather than less likely to openly discuss the desire for assisted death.[14] Hospice and palliative care is not necessarily always an alternative to assisted dying, rather its valuable emphasis upon making the process of dying more in keeping with the patient's own values may, in fact, facilitate frank discussion about euthanasia and assisted suicide.

It is also critical to recognise that the availability of assisted dying is of value to a much wider section of society than will ever, in fact, access it. Discussion about the option of assisted dying may then serve a purpose other than that of hastening death. In the Netherlands, only a minority of the people who formally initiate requests for assistance in dying dies as a result of euthanasia

---

[13] L Van den Block, R Deschepper, J Bilsen, N Bossuyt, V Van Casteren and L Deliens, 'Euthanasia and Other End of Life Decisions and Care Provided in Final Three Months of Life: Nationwide Retrospective Study in Belgium' (2009) 339 *British Medical Journal* b2772.

[14] CF Seale and J Addington-Hall, 'Euthanasia: the Role of Good Care' (1995) 40 *Social Science and Medicine* 581–87.

or assisted suicide.[15] Frances Norwood's anthropological study of people requesting euthanasia in the Netherlands found that most of them did not, in fact, want to die; rather they wanted what she referred to as 'an insurance policy for future suffering'.[16] Amongst her interviewees, what mattered most was knowing that, if necessary, they would be able to avoid the sort of death they feared – commonly the sort of death they had witnessed someone else suffer. In practice then, regardless of whether one ever actually opts for an assisted death, the *prospect* of being able to exercise some control over the dying process may enhance the present quality of life of the terminally ill.

III. THE STATUS QUO IS INDEFENSIBLE

It is also important to acknowledge that a prohibition of assisted dying commonly coexists with a wide range of other lawful practices through which the lives of patients may be shortened, most frequently by the medical profession. In intensive care units, it is relatively common for people to die following the withdrawal of treatment that had been keeping them alive. The use of sedatives and painkilling drugs in end-of-life care is regarded as proper medical treatment, even when it may incidentally hasten a patient's death. Given that there are a number of lawful ways in which patients' lives might be shortened by their doctors, what would be wrong with also permitting doctors to end life quickly and painlessly using a single lethal injection?

Lines are being drawn between lawful and unlawful practices, but I will argue that they are not necessarily always in the right place, and are sometimes hard to defend. When treatment such as artificial nutrition or mechanical ventilation is withdrawn from a patient, he will die from starvation or suffocation, both of which

---

[15] BD Onwuteaka-Philipsen, JKM Gevers, A van der Heide et al, *Evaluation of the Law of Review of Ending of Life on Request and Assisted Suicide* (Amsterdam, ZonMw, 2007).

[16] F Norwood, *The Maintenance of Life: Preventing Social Death Through Euthanasia Talk and End-of-Life Care* (Durham NC, Carolina Academic Press, 2009).

take longer and may be more distressing than the immediate and painless death that would be induced by a fatal injection. Paradoxically then, the lawful means through which a patient's death can be hastened commonly result in more prolonged deaths than the unlawful means.

A. Double Effect

It has long been accepted that doctors are entitled to administer painkilling drugs in quantities which might also hasten death or shorten life. As Devlin J explained in 1957:

> If the first purpose of medicine, the restoration of health, can no longer be achieved, there is still much for a doctor to do, and he is entitled to do all that is proper and necessary to relieve pain and suffering, even if the measures he takes may incidentally shorten life.[17]

This is often referred to as the doctrine of double effect, which has its roots in Roman Catholic moral theology, and more specifically in Thomas Aquinas's reflections on the justification for killing in self-defence. Its function is to distinguish between outcomes which are intended, and outcomes which are merely foreseen as likely, but unintended, consequences of one's conduct. As a person's disease progresses, they may need steadily increasing doses of painkillers, such as diamorphine and morphine, in order to alleviate their pain. When given in sufficient quantities, these drugs can cause respiratory depression and death. According to the doctrine of double effect, a doctor who intends a good consequence (relieving pain) is not guilty of murder just because she foresees, but does not intend, a bad consequence (death).

There is some debate over whether the proper use of opioids will ever, in practice, shorten a patient's life. Many palliative care experts claim that, if used properly, pain-relieving drugs should

---

[17] *R v Adams* (8 April 1957).

never have this effect.[18] But the point is not whether or not high-quality palliative care should ever involve giving life-threatening doses of painkilling drugs. Rather, the point is that – in countries where euthanasia is illegal – it appears to be lawful to do so.

Of course, the doctrine of double effect would not normally relieve a doctor of responsibility for giving drugs that might cause death. If I visit my doctor complaining of mild stomach cramps, it would not be acceptable for him to give me a life-threatening injection of diamorphine, and he could not escape responsibility for my death by pointing to the doctrine of double effect. My doctor could not claim that his intention was merely to relieve my pain, and that my death was a foreseen but unintended side-effect. Death may not be the *principal* purpose of a doctor who administers a potentially lethal dose of painkillers to a terminally ill patient, but he must have decided that the patient's interest in pain relief now outweighs his interest in continued life. It may be true that death is not the intended outcome, but it must have become a tolerable or a reasonable one, otherwise giving drugs that might shorten life would be negligent, if not criminal.

Importantly, while it would be good practice to take the patient's values and beliefs into account when deciding how to manage their pain, the doctrine of double effect does *not* require there to have been a prior request for pain relief that could shorten life. The doctrine of double effect can therefore be invoked to justify conduct which may shorten the life of a patient who lacks capacity, and who may not, in fact, have shared the doctor's view that the relief of their pain is more important to them than being alive.

The doctrine of double effect, in theory then, could permit a doctor to hasten a patient's death provided that he uses analgesic drugs to do so, and provided that he does not 'intend' the result which his medical education, and in particular his understanding of how opioids work, should have taught him was likely, or even

---

[18] I Finlay, 'Dying and Choosing' (2009) 373 *The Lancet* 1840–41; M Ashby, 'The Fallacies of Death Causation in Palliative Care' (1997) *Medical Journal of Australia* 166.

inevitable. Hastening death is acceptable then as long as it also plausibly is intended to relieve pain, and as long as the doctor directs his attention away from the likelihood that the dose he is giving will cause death. If this is acceptable, why not allow death to be hastened using a muscle relaxant drug, and with the open and transparent acknowledgement – as is normal in the law – that if you do something knowing that a particular outcome is 'virtually certain', or even just 'reasonably foreseeable', you should be judged responsible for bringing about that outcome?[19]

B. Terminal Sedation

Various terms are used to describe the use of sedation before death. The terminology can be confusing, and refers to a number of different practices, some of which are temporary responses to a patient's distress, while others may come very close to euthanasia.

Palliative sedation can be intermittent and light, or continuous and deep. It is undoubtedly lawful and may be good medical practice to use sedatives in order to relieve a patient's distress, perhaps because she is having difficulty breathing or swallowing. The level of sedation can be titrated or varied, depending upon the nature and extent of the patient's discomfort. Sometimes only light sedation is needed, and it may be stopped when the patient can be made comfortable without it. If light sedation is insufficient to relieve the patient's suffering, it would be appropriate to give her a higher dose in order to deeply sedate her. Deep sedation, which again is lawful medical treatment, may involve giving a patient sedatives at a dosage where they effectively anaesthetise her into unconsciousness.

In the UK, continuous deep sedation was reported to have preceded 16.5 per cent of all deaths,[20] and a European systematic literature review found that it was sometimes administered to as

---

[19] *R v Woollin* [1999] 1 AC 82, HL.
[20] C Seale, 'End-of-life Decisions in the UK Involving Medical Practitioners' (2009) 23 *Palliative Medicine* 198–204.

many as 50 per cent of patients receiving palliative and hospice care.[21] The intention is to relieve distress and discomfort through sedation, and if the patient is simultaneously hydrated, this is straightforwardly a case of symptom relief, which has little in common with assisted dying.

It is, however, worth noting that the decision to use sedation in order to keep the patient comfortable can be accompanied by a decision to withdraw artificial hydration and nutrition (ANH), with the result that the patient will die. The decision to withhold or withdraw artificial hydration may be taken in order to relieve the distress and discomfort of artificial feeding, and again this would be proper palliative care, the aim of which is to preserve a patient's comfort and dignity, rather than to prolong his life at all costs. Nevertheless it is clear that if a patient is sedated into unconsciousness and *not* simultaneously artificially hydrated, the inevitable result will be her death.

Where the use of sedation in end-of-life care comes closest to euthanasia is when the patient is instantaneously deeply and continuously sedated into a coma, before their life-supporting treatment is withdrawn. Each of the two parts of this process are separately justifiable as ordinary, lawful medical treatment: sedatives are given in order to alleviate discomfort or distress, and once the dying patient is unconscious, the withdrawal of ANH is justifiable because, given that the patient will not regain consciousness, it has become futile. Yet to treat what might be called *terminal sedation* as two separate medical decisions, in order to benefit from their separate legality, is to engage in what Johannes van Delden has referred to as a 'salami slicing technique'.[22] If the decision to opt for terminal sedation is regarded as a *single* medical choice, it is hard to see why it should be more acceptable than giving an injection that contains not just sedatives, but also the means

[21] J Engström, E Bruno, B Holm and O Hellzén, 'Palliative Sedation at End of Life – A Systematic Literature Review' (2007) 11 *European Journal of Oncology Nursing* 26–35.

[22] Johannes J M van Delden, 'Terminal Sedation: Source of a Restless Ethical Debate' (2007) 33 *Journal of Medical Ethics* 187–88.

to end life itself, rather than subsequently relying upon starvation and dehydration to achieve the inevitable outcome – death.

C. 'Do Not Attempt Resuscitation' Orders

It is common for very sick and/or elderly patients' medical notes to contain instructions that, if they should suffer a cardiac arrest, resuscitation should not be attempted. These are known as 'Do Not Resuscitate' or 'Do Not Attempt Resuscitation' (DNAR) orders or codes, and it has been estimated that as many as 80 per cent of patients who die in hospital may have DNAR orders in place.[23] The justification for a prospective decision not to attempt cardio-pulmonary resuscitation is that it can be burdensome – broken ribs, for example, are not uncommon – and, if the patient is close to death anyway, the burdens may outweigh any possible advantages.

While good practice will often be to discuss future resuscitation with the patient, this does not always happen. In fact, while it is relatively common for doctors to discuss DNAR orders with the patient's family, it is unusual to involve the patient herself. The result of not attempting cardio-pulmonary resuscitation may be the patient's death, yet these potentially life-and-death decisions are frequently made without consulting the person whose life is at stake.

In the UK, guidelines issued by the Royal College of Anaesthetists, the Royal College of Physicians, the Intensive Care Society and the Resuscitation Council stress that decisions not to attempt resuscitation may be appropriate when this is the wish of the patient, and also when 'Successful CPR is likely to be followed by a length and quality of life that is not in the best interests of the patient'.[24] If the patient herself is not involved in this judge-

[23] S Aune, J Herlitz and A Bang, 'Characteristics of Patients Who Die in Hospital with no Attempt at Resuscitation' (2005) 65 *Resuscitation* 291–99.

[24] 'Cardiopulmonary Resuscitation: Standards for Clinical Practice and Training, A Joint Statement from the Royal College of Anaesthetists, The Royal College of Physicians of London, The Intensive Care Society and the Resuscitation Council (UK)' (London, Resuscitation Council (UK), 2004). Available at www.resus.org.uk.

ment, and she generally isn't, this necessarily involves other people deciding whether the patient's extended life is likely to be of value to her. Without knowing the patient's own views, there is clearly the potential for subjective and perhaps also discriminatory judgements about the patient's future quality of life to be made. Hakim et al's study of nearly 7000 seriously ill patients, with an average life expectancy of six months, found that comparatively few DNAR orders were written for younger dying patients, whereas the majority of patients over the age of 85 had DNAR orders in their notes.[25]

D. Treatment Withdrawal

It can be lawful to withdraw life-prolonging or sustaining treatment – commonly artificial feeding and mechanical ventilation – both from patients who have mental capacity and from patients who lack capacity. The rules differ depending upon whether the patient is able to request treatment withdrawal themselves, or whether the decision is taken for them by others, but the important point is that, in both cases, a course of action which will result in the patient's death is regarded as lawful medical treatment. In what follows, I shall suggest that in relation to patients both with and without capacity, it is illogical to condone bringing about death by treatment withdrawal while at the same time absolutely prohibiting bringing about death in a quicker and perhaps less distressing way, namely by giving a single, lethal injection.

i. Patients with Mental Capacity

In most jurisdictions, mentally competent adult patients have the right to refuse medical treatment, including life-saving or life-sustaining treatment, for 'rational reasons, irrational reasons or

---

[25] RB Hakim, JM Teno, FE Harrell, WA Knaus, N Wenger, RS Phillips, P Layde, R Califf, AF Connors and J Lynn, 'Factors Associated with do not Resuscitate Orders: Patients' Preferences, Prognoses and Physicians' Judgements' (1996) 125 *Annals of Internal Medicine* 284–93.

no reasons at all.'[26] The consequence of this is that when a patient who wants her life to be brought to an end happens to need medical treatment to keep her alive – a mechanical ventilator, for example – she is entitled to demand that doctors do something which will cause her death.

One of the leading cases in the UK is *Re B (Adult: Refusal of Treatment)*.[27] Ms B was completely paralysed from the neck down. She had respiratory problems, and could not breathe unaided. The clinicians treating her were reluctant to comply with her repeated requests to be removed from the ventilator which was keeping her alive. Ms B sought, and was granted, a court declaration that she had mental capacity and that, as a result, continuing to ventilate her against her wishes was unlawful. As a result of the treating clinicians' unwillingness to cause her death, she was then moved to another hospital, the ventilator was disconnected and she died.

In the US, the courts have vigorously defended the right of a competent adult to determine whether life-prolonging treatment should be initiated or continued. The source of this right has been twofold. First, as in the UK, the courts have pointed to the need for a patient's consent to medical treatment which means that, in the *absence* of the patient's consent to life-sustaining treatment, its provision is unlawful. A long line of cases, approved by the Supreme Court in *Cobbs v Grant,* have held that 'where a doctor performs treatment in the absence of the patient's informed consent, there is an actionable battery. The obvious corollary to this principle is that *a competent adult patient has the legal right to refuse medical treatment*' (my emphasis).[28]

Secondly, the US courts have also suggested that the right to refuse unwanted medical treatment might be grounded in the constitutional right to liberty. In *Cruzan v Director,* Missouri *Department of Health*,[29] Justice O'Connor argued that 'a protected

---

[26] *Re T (Adult: Refusal of Treatment)* [1993] Fam 95.
[27] *Re B (Adult: Refusal of Treatment)* [2002] EWHC 429 (Fam).
[28] *Cobbs v Grant* (1972) 8 Cal 3d 229, 104 Cal Rptr 505, 502 P.2d 1.
[29] *Cruzan v Director,* Missouri *Department of Health* 497 US 261 (1990).

liberty interest in refusing unwanted medical treatment may be inferred from our prior decisions, and that the refusal of artificially delivered food and water is encompassed within that liberty interest.' And in *Washington v Glucksberg*,[30] Chief Justice Rehnquist said that in *Cruzan* the Supreme Court had 'assumed that the Constitution granted competent persons a constitutionally protected right to refuse lifesaving hydration and nutrition'.

In *Bouvia v Superior Court*,[31] the Californian Court of Appeals determined that Elizabeth Bouvia, who was competent and suffered from cerebral palsy, had the right to demand the withdrawal of artificial nutrition and hydration:

> Here Elizabeth Bouvia's decision to forego medical treatment or life-support through a mechanical means belongs to her. It is not a medical decision for her physicians to make. Neither is it a legal question whose soundness is to be resolved by lawyers or judges. It is not a conditional right subject to approval by ethics committees or courts of law. It is a moral and philosophical decision that, being a competent adult, is hers alone.

In an especially moving passage, the Court explained why it was so important that Ms Bouvia should have the right to demand the withdrawal of the nasogastric tube which was keeping her alive:

> Her condition is irreversible. There is no cure for her palsy or arthritis. Petitioner would have to be fed, cleaned, turned, bedded, toileted by others for 15 to 20 years. Although alert, bright, sensitive, perhaps even brave and feisty, she must lie immobile, unable to exist except through physical acts of others. Her mind and spirit may be free to take great flights but she herself is imprisoned and must lie physically helpless subject to the ignominy, embarrassment, humiliation and dehumanizing aspects created by her helplessness. We do not believe it is the policy of this State that all and every life must be preserved against the will of the sufferer. It is incongruous, if not monstrous, for medical practitioners to assert their right to preserve a life that

---

[30] *Washington v Glucksberg* 521 US 702 (1997).
[31] *Bouvia v Superior Court* 179 Cal App 3d 1127, 225 Cal Rptr 297, Cal App 2 Dist,1986.

someone else must live, or, more accurately, endure, for '15 to 20 years'. We cannot conceive it to be the policy of this State to inflict such an ordeal upon anyone.

ii. The Limits of Autonomy

The dominant value in relation to life-ending treatment withdrawal decisions has been autonomy, and the law is absolutely clear that in cases involving treatment refusal, the value of autonomy trumps the value the law attaches to the sanctity of life. Of course, in these cases, the version of autonomy that is being prioritised by the law is not the 'thin', much-criticised version, in which the rational, isolated actor makes decisions about his life without any consideration of how his choices might affect anyone else. On the contrary, the patients in these cases are crucially dependent upon other people, namely healthcare professionals, to comply with their wishes. The decision may be for the patient, but it cannot be realised without assistance.

In the *Ms B* case, the relational consequences of her decision were evident in the evidence given by the treating physicians, who did not feel able to comply with Ms B's wishes because they felt they were being asked to 'kill' her. They had become fond of her, and hoped that she would change her mind. Strictly speaking, once she had withdrawn her consent to being treated they had no right to continue to treat her unlawfully. It is, however, significant that the court endorsed the idea that the healthcare professionals' views, while not determinative, were still worthy of respect. Despite the fact that ventilating her without her consent could amount to an assault, the doctors were not ordered to stop treating her unlawfully and immediately withdraw her from the ventilator. Instead, Ms B was moved to another hospital for the treatment withdrawal, and her subsequent death. Her autonomy may have been the 'trumping' value in this case, but the healthcare professionals' relationship with Ms B was also significant and deserved a degree of respect that would not normally be afforded by the stark finding that she was being treated unlawfully and that this had to stop.

One of the reasons why a narrow, individualistic autonomy model doesn't work as a justification for assisted dying is that one cannot choose an assisted death without implicating and involving at least one other person in that decision. To ask someone else to help bring about one's death is to impose a significant burden upon them. An autonomous individual cannot make and complete a choice for euthanasia or assisted suicide on his own. On the contrary, the whole point is that he needs help to end his life quickly and painlessly.

Treatment withdrawal too, while it is, strictly speaking, a decision for the patient to make on his own, again affects the person who is asked or told to withdraw treatment that is keeping the patient alive. Despite the emotional cost to the 'withdrawer' of treatment, however, once the patient has established their mental competence, that is – in legal terms at least – the end of the matter, and they have the right to have their life brought to an end through the withdrawal of whatever treatment is keeping them alive.

Provided they have mental capacity, questions of whether the person who wishes to refuse life-saving treatment might be suffering from temporary and treatable depression do not arise. Nor are doctors under a duty to investigate whether there might be other, preferable ways to relieve their suffering. No one seems especially concerned that someone who refuses life-prolonging treatment might wrongly believe herself to be a burden to others. Regardless of whether her suffering is likely to be both temporary and short-lived, a person is still entitled to make a decision which will lead to her death. Indeed, it is not even necessary for someone who refuses life-prolonging treatment to establish that they are suffering at all. You do not need to have a good reason to refuse unwanted life-prolonging medical treatment.

In short then, when the decision to have one's life brought to an end can be accomplished by a *refusal* of treatment, there are virtually no safeguards to ensure that the person's wish is settled, voluntary and justified by the circumstances in which they find themselves. Their decision can be foolish and misguided, but if it is competently made, it is binding and must be respected. We allow people to make a definitive choice for death by demanding the removal of a tube delivering nourishment or oxygen, but not by asking for a needle containing lethal medication to be inserted into their vein. If we can be certain enough about questions like the person's capacity to make a decision that will result in their death, and the voluntariness of their choice, in the former case, surely it is illogical to argue that we could never be sufficiently certain about exactly the same matters in the latter case?

Some people object to assisted dying because they think it would involve us accepting that some lives are not worth living. Yet in the case of Ms B, she had undoubtedly decided that her life was not worth living, and there was nothing that the law could do to stop her getting her way. Others argue that palliative care is always able to relieve suffering at the end of life, and must be preferred to a quicker, medically induced death. Yet even if palliative care might have radically improved Ms B's life, she had a right to demand that her life be brought to an end by the removal of the ventilator that was keeping her alive.

iii.   Treatment Withdrawal from Patients who Lack Capacity

The tests that doctors and the courts must use when determining what treatment, if any, to give to a patient who lacks capacity are the best interests test (used in the UK), and the substituted judgement test (more commonly invoked in the US). At first sight there would appear to be an important difference between these tests: in the UK, we ask, paternalistically, what would be *best for the patient*, whereas in the US, we ask what *the patient would have wanted*. But in fact any difference between these tests is more apparent than real. In the UK, the patient's values, wishes and beliefs are a key factor in the best interests assessment, which is undoubtedly *not* limited to their objectively assessed clinical interests. Hence while the doctor's judgement about what is medically 'best' for the patient is relevant, so too is what the patient would have wanted. Similarly, in the US, in the absence of a clear statement of the patient's wishes, the substituted judgement test will be influenced by the presumption that the patient would want what experts consider the best medical treatment for her condition.

Of course, both the best interests test and the substituted judgement test will usually demand that patients are given life-prolonging treatment. It is only in extreme situations that positively withdrawing treatment that is keeping someone alive could be said to be either 'in their best interests' or 'what they would have wanted'. These tend to be cases in which the patient is permanently comatose and there is no prospect of them regaining consciousness. An example might be patients who are in what is known as a permanent vegetative state (PVS).

In the US, in keeping with the substituted judgement test, the courts have asked what the patient him- or herself would have wanted. For PVS patients, this may present a problem, because PVS is commonly precipitated by a sudden event, such as an accident in which the patient suffers catastrophic head injuries. The patient frequently has no warning of their impending incapacity. Unlike patients suffering from progressive diseases, like cancer or HIV/AIDS, these are not patients who have had the opportunity to engage in advance care planning in which they might specify what they do and do not want to happen to them if they lose capacity. As a result, it is sometimes difficult to be certain what they would have wanted.

This was the root of the problem in the case of Theresa (or Terri) Schiavo, who had lapsed into a permanent vegetative state after she suffered a cardiac arrest in 1990. Eight years later, her husband Michael petitioned a Florida court to remove her feeding tube. He claimed that she would not want to have been kept alive in a permanent vegetative state, but her parents disagreed. What followed was an extraordinarily unedifying and prolonged legal spectacle, in which Ms Schiavo's feeding tube was removed on several occasions, on the order of a number of courts, only to be subsequently reinserted. After seven years of bitter and acrimonious litigation between her husband, who said she would not have wanted to be kept alive in a PVS, and her parents, who took a different view, Ms Schiavo finally died, 15 years after she had lost consciousness.

The leading case in the UK is *Airedale NHS Trust v Bland*,[32] where the House of Lords decided that it would be lawful to withdraw artificial nutrition and hydration (ANH) from Tony Bland, who had been in a permanent vegetative state since suffering catastrophic head injuries at the Hillsborough football stadium disaster in 1989. The Law Lords were bound by law to apply the 'best interests' test in determining what treatment should be given to Tony Bland, but, as several of them pointed out, it could be argued that the best interests test is not especially helpful when the patient has effectively ceased to have any interests at all.

The House of Lords unanimously decided that it would be lawful for Airedale NHS Trust to withdraw ANH from Tony Bland, with the result that he would die. In order to authorise this course of action, it was first necessary to characterise ANH as medical treatment, rather than basic care, such as washing a patient and giving them oral hydration, which cannot be withdrawn. Secondly, in order to authorise treatment withdrawal, the Lords had to describe the positive removal of the feeding tube as an omission, and not an action. If the removal of the tube had instead been acknowledged to be an action, it would have been hard to avoid the conclusion that this would have satisfied both the *mens rea* (intention to kill) and the *actus reus* (proof of conduct and proof that the conduct caused death) of murder.

Labelling treatment withdrawal as an omission in this case was an example of what might be called 'backwards reasoning', in which a judge decides what outcome they wish to reach, and then finds a line of legal reasoning which enables them to secure this result. The legality of treatment withdrawal in these circumstances depended upon it being an omission. Some members of the House of Lords were satisfied that this decision was grounded in a meaningful difference between acts and omissions, whereas Lord Mustill admitted that he found the distinction 'morally and

---

[32] *Airedale NHS Trust v Bland* [1993] AC 789, HL.

intellectually dubious'. Lord Mustill was also remarkably frank about the 'acute unease' he felt about 'adopting this way through the legal and ethical maze':

> The conclusion that the declarations can be upheld depends crucially on a distinction drawn by the criminal law between acts and omissions . . . The acute unease which I feel about adopting this way through the legal and ethical maze is I believe due in an important part to the sensation that however much the terminologies may differ the ethical status of the two courses of action is for all relevant purposes indistinguishable. By dismissing this appeal I fear that your Lordships' House may only emphasise the distortions of a legal structure which is already both morally and intellectually misshapen. Still, the law is there and we must take it as it stands.

Obviously, subjecting a patient who lacks capacity to futile or burdensome treatment may not be in their best interests, but it is not clear that ANH is either futile or burdensome for patients who are in a permanent vegetative state. Treatment is futile when it can no longer achieve its intended objective. There comes a point for patients in the final stages of terminal cancer, for example, when giving them chemotherapy would be futile because it can no longer deliver any beneficial effect, and at that stage, it is more appropriate to provide palliative care in order to relieve pain and make the patient comfortable. Delivering ANH to a PVS patient can continue to achieve its intended objective – keeping the patient alive – for many years. To say that it is futile must be to make a rather different claim, namely that *keeping the patient alive* is now futile because being alive, which the treatment can undoubtedly continue to deliver, is no longer a benefit to them.

Nor is ANH burdensome for a PVS patient who will be completely unaware of any discomfort associated with being fed through a tube. In short, artificial feeding is not futile (it does what it is intended to do), nor is it burdensome to the PVS patient to keep him alive for many years. Yet the law has recognised that there are times when being kept alive is not in a patient's best interests. It is hard to avoid the conclusion that in these cases the law is in fact recognising that death can be preferable to continued existence in a permanently vegetative state. If this is the case, however, why does the law insist that the only lawful way in which that end can be achieved is by dehydrating and starving the patient until they die? Why not allow exactly the same end to be achieved more quickly through giving the patient a single lethal injection? Lord Browne-Wilkinson in the *Bland* case admitted to finding it difficult to answer this question:

> How can it be lawful to allow a patient to die slowly, though painlessly, over a period of weeks from lack of food but unlawful to produce his immediate death by a lethal injection, thereby saving his family from yet another ordeal to add to the tragedy that has already struck them? I find it difficult to find a moral answer to that question. But it is undoubtedly the law.

A counter-argument might be that removing the feeding tube does not kill a patient in a permanent vegetative state, rather it fails to deliver food to him, and he dies because he has an underlying condition which prevents him from being able to feed himself. This suggests, however, that standing back and watching someone die from an underlying and easily treatable condition is acceptable behaviour for doctors, which in the normal course of events, it is not. If a patient is admitted to hospital suffering from acute dehydration, it would not be acceptable for the doctors to say 'well we could easily put him on a saline drip, but if we don't, he will simply die from his underlying condition, and that is no concern of ours.' It would only be acceptable to withdraw or withhold hydration and nutrition from a patient when causing their death has become acceptable. But it is not the fact that this is accomplished by treatment withdrawal which, on its own, makes causing death acceptable.

It would be a mistake to imply that decisions to withdraw life-prolonging treatment from patients who lack capacity are always made by courts, following painstaking consideration of the particular circumstances of the individual patient. On the contrary, it is relatively common for people admitted to intensive care units after suffering massive strokes, for example, or catastrophic brain injuries, to be removed from the ventilators which are keeping them alive. It is undoubtedly good practice in such cases to con-sult the patient's family about what he would have wanted, but this does not always happen in practice. In her 2011 report into failings in the care of elderly people in the British NHS, one of the Ombudsman's 10 case studies involved a decision being made to switch off the patient's life support with no regard to the feel-ings of the family, let alone any investigation into the wishes of the person who died:

> Miss C told the nurse that they were going to make a phone call and stated expressly that the life support was not to be switched off as she was coming back to sit with her father. She was still hopeful of a recovery. Miss C later told us that, had she known her father was going to have his life support switched off, she would have wanted to help him *'go peacefully after being battered by so many medical procedures and surrounded by strangers'*. However, she and her mother returned to find that Mr C's ventilator had already been switched off. Miss C felt that *'the staff decided that we had been given as much time as we were allowed'*. Mr C was pronounced dead at 10.25pm . . . As his daughter said later *'We would have liked the opportunity to have the peace of mind of sitting with my father and of praying for him. I have the feeling that I failed my father'*. [33]

Again, it is noteworthy that death-inducing treatment withdrawal is subject to few if any safeguards to protect the vulnerable and to make sure that it is consistent with their values and beliefs. The argument that legalised assisted dying would represent a unique opportunity to mistreat the vulnerable is clearly misplaced.

iv. The Difference Between Killing and Letting Die

The line the law draws between treatment withdrawal, which is normal medical treatment, and euthanasia, which could amount to murder and be punishable by life imprisonment, means that everything turns on the difference between killing and letting die,

---

[33] 'Report of the Health Service Ombudsman on Ten Investigations into NHS Care of Older People' (London, Department of Health, 2011) available at www.ombudsman.org.uk/care-and-compassion/introduction.

or between acts and omissions. Given that both courses of conduct will lead to the patient's death, do the different bodily movements involved in injecting someone with lethal medication, and removing a feeding tube, justify these completely different legal responses? It will be my contention that the differences between the two sorts of conduct, while not non-existent, are in this case insufficient to bear the moral weight that is placed upon them by the law.

If someone breaks into a neonatal intensive care ward and deliberately removes all the babies from the ventilators and feeding tubes which are keeping them alive, this is not acceptable conduct because it involves letting the babies die, rather than killing them. 'Letting die' by removing a ventilator or a feeding tube could clearly amount to murder. It is, I would argue, not the fact that Ms B was removed from a ventilator that made deliberate conduct which caused her death legitimate, rather it is the fact that this represented her settled, voluntary and competent choice. In the case of Tony Bland, again it is not the fact that he died from dehydration and starvation that made causing his death acceptable behaviour.

A patient who is in the final stages of cancer and suffering unbearably might beg his doctor to put him out of his misery and end his life. According to James Rachels,[34] the doctor has three options. He can give the patient a lethal injection, but this would be murder and is forbidden. Alternatively, assuming the patient requires some sort of life-sustaining treatment, he can cease to provide that treatment, and the patient will die. Or he can prolong life 'until the bitter end'. Both of the latter courses of action are lawful, even though each will, in fact, prolong this man's suffering. Death from treatment withdrawal, and from letting nature take its course, will inevitably take longer than the death that would result from a lethal injection. What reason could there be to prefer a course of action – treatment withdrawal – which has exactly the same goal (death), and result (death), but which will achieve that

---

[34] J Rachels, *The End of Life* (Oxford, Oxford University Press, 1986).

result more slowly, thus potentially exposing the dying patient to more pain and distress?

One reason might be to do with causation. In the first case, the lethal injection is the *cause* of the patient's death, whereas in the second case, the patient's death is caused by their underlying disease, which has given rise to their need for life-sustaining treatment. And there are undoubtedly times when it is plausible to say that withholding medical treatment means the patient simply dies from their underlying condition. If antibiotics are withheld from a patient who needs them to treat a gangrenous infection, it makes sense to say that the cause of the patient's death is gangrene. Relying on causation in this way is less plausible, however, where a patient with terminal cancer is dependent upon artificial nutrition and hydration (ANH), and is being fed through a tube. The direct cause of death, in these circumstances, is dehydration and starvation, rather than cancer.

The person who brings about death by dehydration and starvation cannot avoid moral responsibility for that death because the person who needed to be fed was already extremely ill. If a patient who wants to go on living is being temporarily fed by a feeding tube, a sadistic doctor who removes the tube could not claim that the patient simply died from his pre-existing condition. On the contrary, the sadistic doctor has deliberately caused the patient's death. Again, we cannot point to the difference between treatment withdrawal and euthanasia as a convenient shorthand for the difference between acceptable and unacceptable conduct. Treatment withdrawal is sometimes very wrong indeed, and conversely, it could be argued that euthanasia would, in certain circumstances, be a legitimate response to a patient's intolerable suffering.

Others might argue that the difference between killing/letting die reflects the important moral distinction between positively harming someone, and failing to help them; and of course, sometimes there is a clear difference between these two courses of action, in terms of both causation and responsibility for the outcome. Not giving money to a charity which helps save lives in developing countries fails to help people who might have benefited from the donation, but it would be unthinkable to prosecute non-donors for murder. In contrast, if someone deliberately poisons a consignment of formula milk, they are undoubtedly the primary cause of – and bear moral responsibility for – the deaths of babies who were fed with the poisoned milk.

But while it is easy to think of examples when the moral difference between not helping and positively harming is fairly clear, in the case of a doctor standing over a patient's bed and making a choice between removing a tube and delivering a lethal injection, it is not self-evident that there is any difference at all, in terms of both causation of, and moral responsibility for, the patient's death. The lack of difference is especially stark when we consider the lawfulness of 'terminal sedation', discussed earlier. If the doctor is allowed to give an injection (unquestionably an action) containing sedatives that will induce a coma, and is then entitled to withdraw the patient's feeding tube, thus causing her death, it is hard to see why giving an injection which contains both a sedative to induce a coma *and* a muscle relaxant to stop breathing is regarded as an entirely different course of action – namely murder – and is punishable by life imprisonment.

What makes the doctor's conduct acceptable is not whether he causes death by an omission or an action. Both can be very wrong indeed, and both can, in certain limited circumstances, be acceptable. In the unusual and restricted circumstances in which it would be acceptable to cause death by an omission, it is hard to see why reaching the same inevitable result in a quicker and less protracted way would subvert the foundations of medical ethics. Once the decision 'for death' has been taken, the means chosen to achieve that end should promote the patient's dignity and reflect the values that were important to them during their life. Of course, that means that someone who objected to euthanasia should have their wishes respected, but if it euthanasia would be consistent with their known views, and especially if they have made those views clearly and consistently known to those involved in their care, to insist they die a longer, more distressing death in order to preserve the integrity of the dubious – or as

Lord Mustill put it 'intellectually misshapen' – legal distinction between acts and omissions is absurd.

E. Exporting the 'Problem' of Assisted Suicide

Citizens who live in countries where assisted dying is unlawful can and do travel to Dignitas's clinics in Switzerland in order to access assisted suicide. In addition to the 'assistance' provided by Dignitas volunteers, people who travel to Switzerland in order to die, most commonly from other European countries, are almost always also 'assisted' by friends or family, who might book an air-line or train ticket or accompany them to Zurich. They are also nearly always 'assisted' by healthcare professionals who will be asked to prepare a copy of their medical notes for them to take with them. Despite assisted suicide being a criminal offence in the UK, punishable by up to 14 years in prison, none of the doctors, relatives or partners of the more than 100 UK citizens who have died in Dignitas clinics so far has faced prosecution.

In addition to the expense of travelling to Switzerland, assisted suicide in a Dignitas clinic costs approximately €4000. The 'Swiss option' is therefore not available to everyone. Those who cannot afford a Swiss assisted suicide, or who do not know about it, are excluded. People also have to go to Zurich while they are still fit enough to travel, meaning that many die sooner than they might otherwise have preferred to, and they cannot die in their own home. As Dr Anne Turner, who suffered from progressive supra-nuclear palsy, and went to Dignitas accompanied by her children in 2006, explained,

> In order to ensure that I am able to swallow the medication that will kill me, I have to go to Switzerland before I am totally incapacitated and unable to travel. If I knew that when things got so bad I would be able to request assisted suicide in Britain, then I would not have to die before I am completely ready to do so.[35]

[35]   S O'Neill, 'Why a Retired GP Chose to End her Life Seven Years before Time' *The Times* (25 January 2006).

It is also by no means clear that Switzerland will continue to offer a relatively simple way around the law, in particular for European citizens. Several unsuccessful attempts have been made to change the law to prohibit foreign citizens from joining Swiss right to die societies. There was a substantial majority in favour of continuing to permit foreigners' access to assisted suicide in a 2011 referendum, but it is clearly possible that the Swiss 'safety valve' may be closed in the future.

In addition, the safeguards in place in Switzerland are not necessarily as rigorous as one might wish a carefully drafted assisted dying law to be. The Swiss have not specifically taken steps to legalise assisted suicide; rather, according to the Swiss Penal Code, it is a crime only if the motive is 'selfish'. All that needs to be established, therefore, is that the person who assisted the suicide acted from compassion. This is a fairly minimal requirement, and although Swiss right to die societies impose their own more rigorous requirements, the law itself contains none of the safeguards – such as psychiatric assessment and a palliative and social support filter – which should, I will argue later, be part of a well-crafted assisted dying law.

In short, anyone who is determined to die at the time of their choosing can access assisted suicide by travelling to Switzerland. But this has multiple disadvantages – earlier deaths, fewer safeguards and people must die in a foreign country, rather than in their own home – and no advantages, unless permitting countries to maintain a prohibition on assisted suicide, while allowing their richer dying citizens to circumvent it relatively easily, is regarded as a benefit.

F. The Euthanasia/Assisted Suicide 'Underground' and the Benefits of Regulation

It is important to remember that the choice is not between legalisation – where assisted dying happens in an open and transparent way – and illegality, where we can be certain that it will never happen. Rather, the illegality of euthanasia and assisted suicide may instead mean that it is practised 'underground'. An analogy might be drawn with the termination of pregnancy before abortion became a lawful medical procedure. When abortion was a crime, this did not mean that women never terminated their unwanted pregnancies. Rather, it meant that they did so in often insanitary and dangerous circumstances.

We know that in countries where assisted dying is unlawful, doctors have helped their patients to die, but they do so under the threat of criminal prosecution and imprisonment, and as a result, assisted deaths happen without any safeguards at all – such as a second opinion or psychiatric assessment. In Roger Magnusson's study of the 'euthanasia underground', he discovered shockingly poor practices: in one case a doctor injected a young man on the first occasion they met, despite concerns from close friends that the patient was depressed.[36] In another case the patient brought his death forward in order not to interfere with the doctor's holiday plans. In comparison with legalised assisted dying, 'underground euthanasia' may be much more dangerous for patients.

Of course, the fact that something bad happens outside of the law is not a good reason for legalising it. If we believe that doctors always act wrongly when they help patients to die, then not only should such assistance be criminalised, but we should do our best to ensure that doctors who flout the prohibition are detected and prosecuted. So it is not the existence of a euthanasia underground in itself that lends weight to the argument that assisted dying should be legalised. Rather my point is that given that illegality leads to *worse* assisted deaths than would happen under restricted conditions of legality, if we think assisted dying is sometimes justifiable – as I hope to establish here – then it is *regulated* assisted dying which should be preferred.

The internet has added a new dimension to the question of what happens when lawful assistance with suicide is not available. Depressed individuals may access effective community support networks through the web, but they can also visit sites which

---

[36] R Magnusson, 'Euthanasia: Above Ground, Below Ground' (2004) 30 *Journal of Medical Ethics* 441–46.

provide detailed information about how to commit suicide, and even in some cases encouragement to do so. If patients who want to die can talk openly and frankly with their doctor about their options, they may be less likely to rely solely on the information they find on the internet. Patients who seek advice from the internet on how to end their lives may botch the attempt and be left in a worse state than before. And it is so obvious as to barely need stating that the internet contains no safeguards at all to protect the vulnerable.

We also know that it is not uncommon for patients who desperately want to end their lives to simply stop eating, and effectively starve themselves to death. In one survey of nurses working in palliative care, 41 per cent had cared for at least one patient who had chosen to stop eating and drinking in order to hasten their death.[37] Their reasons for doing so were 'a readiness to die, the belief that continuing to live was pointless, an assessment of the quality of life as poor, a desire to die at home, and a desire to control the circumstances of death'. Although death from self-starvation and dehydration can be peaceful, it can also be protracted and uncomfortable – both for the patient and for her carers, who must stand by and watch the person's body slowly wither away – and there are, once again, few safeguards to protect the vulnerable.

If self-starvation, botched suicide attempts and a euthanasia underground lead patients to die worse deaths than they would under a controlled, regulated system of lawful assisted suicide or euthanasia, then provided we think that assisted dying is sometimes an understandable response to extreme suffering, it is clear that a regulated system is capable of offering more protection to the vulnerable than prohibition.

---

[37] L Ganzini, ER Goy, LL Miller, TA Harvath, A Jackson and MA Delori, 'Nurses' Experiences with Hospice Patients Who Refuse Food and Fluids to Hasten Death' (2003) 349 *New England Journal of Medicine* 359–65; TE Quill, B Lo and DW Brock, 'Palliative Options of Last Resort: A Comparison of Voluntarily Stopping Eating and Drinking, Terminal Sedation, Physician-Assisted Suicide, and Voluntary Active Euthanasia' (1997) 278 *Journal of the American Medical Association* 2099–104.

IV. WHY MIGHT ANYONE THINK WE SHOULDN'T TRY?

Opponents of assisted dying tend to argue that legalisation would be either wrong in principle, and/or a dangerous step to take. When evaluating their arguments, it is important to remember that because opponents of assisted dying believe that *nobody* should have access to assisted dying, they have to explain not just why it is incompatible with their personal beliefs, but also why other people, whose values are different, should be bound by a prohibition with which they disagree.

A. The Sanctity and Value of Life

It is sometimes said that assisted dying is incompatible with the sanctity of human life, or with the principle that all human life is intrinsically valuable. There are two strands to this claim. First, it could derive from the religious belief that life is not ours to dispose of as we please. For a human being to choose the moment of her death, and to take active steps to bring it about is, according to this view, to usurp God's monopoly upon the power to give and to take life. Suicide, it has been said, is a rebellion against God, which not only takes his place in exercising the power of life and death, but also fails to recognise the responsibilities that come with the gift of life.

This version of the sanctity of life objection to assisted dying can be dispensed with relatively easily as a determinant of public policy in a secular society. The idea that God alone should have the power to decide the moment of an individual's death may be of utmost importance to some people, and would undoubtedly determine whether they would request euthanasia themselves, or participate in its provision. It does not, however, justify restricting the choices available to others who do not share these religious beliefs. People of faith may believe that they are stewards of God, accountable to him for their lives and how they use them, but many others do not believe this. Suicide is indeed a tragedy, for the person who dies and for the people who love him, but, for a non-believer, this is not because he has encroached upon God's territory.

It could also be argued that God's monopoly on determining the moment of death has already been substantially usurped by modern medicine. The medical profession determines the time of death through the removal of life-sustaining treatment or the giving of life-threatening doses of painkilling drugs. Moreover, medical treatment is generally directed towards *impeding* the natural progression of disease in order to prolong life long after it might, without artificial interference, have come to an end.

The second version of the sanctity of life objection to assisted dying is that if we can imagine circumstances in which death might rationally be preferred to life, we must believe that some lives are essentially not worth living. This involves making a quality of life judgement that some believe to be irreconcilable with the principle that all lives are of equal value, or with the respect which is due to every member of society, regardless of how sick or disabled they might be. The idea that assisted dying must be prohibited in order to avoid making qualitative judgements about whether a patient's life is worth living is worthy of more discussion, although it too is ultimately unconvincing.

Richard Harries has argued that acceding to someone's request for assisted dying would not necessarily be the most compassionate response to their distress, since it would send them the message that we agree with them that it would be better if they ceased to exist:

> In agreeing to allow a person in her distress to kill herself with the help of a doctor, would we in fact be sending a subliminal message to her that we no longer really want her with us, that she is becoming too much of a burden for us?[38]

Instead, Harries suggests that a preferable response might be 'a continuing re-affirmation of your love and care for her [which]

---

[38] R Harries, *Questions of Life and Death: Christian Faith and Medical Intervention* (London, Society for Promoting Christian Knowledge, 2010) 109.

would make her feel that – despite everything – it was still worthwhile continuing in this life for the time being'.[39] The prohibition on assisted suicide, according to Harries, 'implicitly make[s] the point that everyone in our society, in whatever state of mental or physical distress, is of value'.[40]

But accepting that someone's life has ceased to benefit them is not the same as saying they have no worth. The children and partners who have accompanied people they love to Switzerland for their assisted suicides have not done so because they believed that their parent or spouse has ceased to be a valuable human being. On the contrary, the desire to be there when someone we love dies and to be able to comfort them in their final days and hours, is prompted by love and compassion, and does not entail subscribing to the view that the person's life has become worthless.

I agree with Richard Harries that a request for assisted dying should prompt us to investigate other ways in which the person's anguish can be eased. It may be that with better care and support, the person's desire to die will recede; but this is an argument for a robust filter on access to assisted dying – what I shall call a 'social support' filter – rather than a reason to absolutely prohibit euthanasia and assisted suicide.

It is also important to be absolutely clear that not everyone experiences the loss of control that prompts some patients' requests for assisted dying as undignified and degrading. Some people who are profoundly physically incapacitated and dependent nevertheless gain considerable meaning and value from their lives. It is crucial to recognise that people differ, and what is tolerable for one person may not be tolerable for someone else. There are profoundly sick and dependent people who would not seek an assisted death under any circumstances, and they deserve to be treated with the utmost care and respect. My point is that the patient herself is the expert here, and the fact that disabled and sick people have different views about what it means for their lives to go well – or to meet some minimum threshold of tolerability –

[39] ibid 110.
[40] ibid 121.

is a reason to respect this diversity, rather than to force those who would prefer to have an assisted death to have to endure instead the suffering that they are desperate to avoid.

James Rachels asks us to imagine that we are given a choice between two deaths. If we opt for the first, we die quietly and painlessly, at the age of 80, after being given a lethal injection.[41] The second death involves us dying a few days later, at the age of 'eighty plus a few days', but from an affliction which is so terrible that we spend those last few days howling like a dog, with our family standing helplessly by. I am prepared to believe that some people's religious faith would lead them to prefer the second option, but many people, basing their decision upon their own interests and those of their family, would undoubtedly be likely to opt for the first death. Yet in countries where assisted dying is unlawful, the peaceful death is absolutely prohibited, with the law permitting only the agonising one.

Certainly, if we were making the choice between these two deaths on behalf of a much loved, elderly pet cat, it is hard to imagine that anyone would believe that forcing him to endure the second death would be the more compassionate or ethical choice. On the contrary, when it comes to animals, most people accept that euthanasia is not only justifiable, but also often the right thing to do.

One justification for treating animals and human beings differently might be that, for animals, the dying process cannot contain anything other than the physical experience of suffering. For animals, dying is not an opportunity for them to reflect upon their life, and to say goodbye. The claim that is sometimes made in relation to humans, namely that dying can be a positive experience, does not make sense when one contemplates the death of a pet cat. He is suffering and we want to do all we can to relieve his pain and distress, by, if necessary, having him 'put down.' But again, while it is undoubtedly true that the process of dying is meaningful for some people, involving 'reconciliation with the last phase of life',[42] for

---

[41] Rachels, n 34 above.
[42] Maaike et al, n 11 above.

others it is simply ghastly. It may be right that it can be important for human beings to come to terms with the fact that they are dying. The human urge to talk about love, and to express it in the face of death is both powerful and cathartic. More prosaically, it can be important for human beings, but clearly not cats, to ensure that they have made a will and given instructions for their funeral. But even if human beings generally do have a rather special need for resolution at the end of their lives, this does not justify forcing someone to suffer intolerably when they have reached the point at which they are ready to die and they just want their suffering to stop.

John Keown has suggested that we should never endorse someone's 'misguided' judgement that their life is no longer worth living,[43] and of course I would agree with him that where someone's judgement is indeed misguided, it would be profoundly wrong to help them end their life. Someone who encourages a depressed teenager to commit suicide by 'egging them on' in an internet chatroom has committed an egregious and repulsive act. But Keown assumes that the judgement that life is no longer worth living is a product of a person's 'depression or pain or loneliness',[44] rather than reflecting their considered, settled and rational view that they have had enough and want to die. While opponents of euthanasia are entitled to believe that their own lives will be worth living regardless of how much suffering they entail, for others there comes a point – as we know from their testimonies – when life has become an intolerable burden, and when death would come as a welcome release. In such circumstances, their desire to end their life is only 'misguided' if we think either that suffering, no matter how terrible, must always be endured, or if we simply do not believe their claim that their suffering has become unbearable. It seems cruel to force someone to endure suffering they find intolerable, and condescending to disbelieve them when they claim to be suffering so much.

---

[43] J Keown, 'Mr Marty's Muddle: A Superficial and Selective Case for Euthanasia in Europe' (2006) 32 *Journal of Medical Ethics* 29–33.

[44] ibid.

If the claim is that we should never endorse a patient's view that their life no longer has any value to them, remember also that we already allow competent adult patients to make this sort of judgement provided that they happen to need life-prolonging medical treatment. If a patient who wants to end her life, because she misguidedly believes it is no longer worth living, happens to be connected to a ventilator or a feeding tube, doctors are not merely under a duty to stand aside and do nothing, rather they must positively remove the device which is keeping the patient alive, and thus are effectively under a duty to deliberately hasten the patient's death.

In relation to PVS patients, there is, surely, an important difference between simply being alive, and having a life which is worth living. For many people, merely existing as a live human being is not enough to make their life worth living. If I am run over by a bus tomorrow and lapse into a permanent vegetative state, I do not want to be kept alive. There is nothing that I would value about being alive in a permanently comatose state: it is not a life and it is not living in any meaningful sense. If someone was to ask me what is valuable about my life, I would talk about my friends, my family, my work and the things I enjoy doing. I would not say that what matters is that I am a functioning biological organism. Of course, being a functioning biological organism is necessary in order for me to enjoy the things that give me pleasure in life, but it is not sufficient, on its own, to make my life valuable to me. There is nothing independently valuable about being alive, other than that it enables me to live a life. A person who is in a permanent vegetative state is alive in a biological sense, but she may not be leading a life which has any value to her. Theresa Schiavo's gravestone is explicit that she had 'departed this earth' some 15 years before her body, as a functioning human organism, ceased to exist:

Schiavo, Theresa Marie, Beloved Wife.

Born December 3 1963, Departed this earth February 26 1990, At peace March 31 2005

I kept my promise.

B. Effect on Doctor–Patient Relationship

A different argument against legalisation is that it would damage the integrity of the medical profession and have a negative impact upon the doctor–patient relationship. There are two interrelated aspects to this argument. First, from the point of view of the patient, it might be argued that knowing your doctor could legally kill you would reduce patient trust, especially among elderly and disabled patients. Whether or not patients share the view that legalisation of assisted dying would diminish their trust in the medical profession is, however, unclear. While we should generally be sceptical of opinion poll evidence, since so much depends on the question asked, a 2004 poll found that 70 per cent of those asked said the legalisation of assisted suicide would not affect their trust in doctors, while 9 per cent would trust doctors more and 9 per cent would trust doctors less.[45]

Secondly, from the point of view of the doctor, if 'killing' were to become a treatment option, the ethical foundations of the medical profession would be undermined. Just as we submit our naked bodies and intimate secrets to doctors, safe in the knowledge that their professional codes of ethics prohibit them from engaging in sexual conduct with us or broadcasting embarrassing details about our health, so – the argument goes – we need to believe that the medical profession will never use its knowledge about fatal doses of drugs in order to kill us. Like the principle of patient confidentiality and the rules about sexual impropriety, the prohibition of euthanasia protects the medical profession's standing as a fundamentally ethical profession, and this in turn fosters patients' trust in their doctors.

It is not, however, clear that what patients fear most at the end of their lives is the prospect of doctors helping them to die prematurely. On the contrary, we know from surveys about patients' interest in making advance directives or 'living wills' that many

---

[45] Select Committee on the Assisted Dying for the Terminally Ill Bill, *Assisted Dying for the Terminally Ill Bill – First Report* (London, Parliament, 2005) 77.

elderly people fear going into hospital because they are worried about the 'overzealous use of life-sustaining procedures . . . which would just prolong their suffering and compromise their dignity and quality of life'.[46] Far from being tempted to persuade their patients to opt for euthanasia in order to 'unblock' hospital beds, the much more compelling temptation for doctors is to do everything humanly possible to postpone death.

Ignoring the patient's own perspective, and refusing to accept the validity of her preference for an assisted death, seems a peculiar way of fostering that patient's trust in the health care professionals responsible for her care. Earlier I pointed to evidence that most people who express an interest in assisted dying are looking for a 'hypothetical exit plan' or 'an insurance policy against future suffering'. Most of them do not want to die now. Knowing that euthanasia or assisted suicide could be an option in the future operates as a kind of 'comfort blanket' which, by eliminating their anxiety about the dying process that might lie ahead, can enhance their present quality of life. If the future availability of assisted dying offers comfort and support to patients who will never actually seek an assisted death, again patient trust may be enhanced by knowing that your doctor really will be able to do all he can to help you if your suffering becomes desperate and unendurable.

Unlike other rules which govern the ethical practice of medicine, it is not possible to make a case that the prohibition of euthanasia shouldn't apply in exceptional circumstances. And it is this fact, rather than the existence of a general rule against killing, that is especially interesting. In relation to other ethical principles, it is usually possible to argue against their application in a particular case if the facts offer sufficiently compelling grounds to make an exception for this individual. The principle of patient confidentiality, for example, does not apply where there is a risk of serious harm, either to the patient herself or to another person, sufficient to justify disclosure. Exceptions can be made to other

---

[46] M Eisemann and J Richter, 'Relationships between Various Attitudes towards Self-Determination in Health Care with Special Reference to an Advance Directive' (1999) 25 *Journal of Medical Ethics* 37–41.

basic ethical principles if countervailing considerations are more important in the exceptional circumstances that have arisen. Yet however compelling an individual patient's reasons for wanting her doctor to help her to die, and however sympathetic a doctor might be to her request, assisted dying remains illegal.

But while the prohibition of euthanasia is in theory without exceptions, it is noteworthy that, in practice, successful prosecutions are unusual. There may be an absolute rule prohibiting doctors from giving their patients lethal injections, but it is also very unlikely that a doctor who helps a patient to die, at her request, will face life imprisonment. Prosecutions are rare, and convictions rarer still. In one of the only UK cases to result in a successful prosecution, Dr Nigel Cox had given his patient Mrs Lilian Boyes a dose of potassium chloride that was more than enough to kill her.[47] It was difficult to avoid the conclusion that he had intended to end her life, and since potassium chloride is not a painkiller, it would not have been possible to argue that his intention was instead to relieve her pain. Mrs Boyes was 70 years old and terminally ill; she had rheumatoid arthritis, gastric ulcers, gangrene and body sores, and she suffered from extreme pain, which could not be controlled with painkilling drugs. There was evidence that she had repeatedly asked Dr Cox, a consultant rheumatologist who had been treating her for the last 13 years, and others to kill her. Because Mrs Boyes's body had been cremated, the cause of death could not be proved with sufficient certainty, so Dr Cox was prosecuted for *attempted* murder. Given that there was clear evidence that he had injected her with a life-ending dosage of potassium chloride, his conviction was inevitable; however it is noteworthy that he did not go to prison, but instead was given a 12-month suspended prison sentence. Nor was he struck off the medical register; after a formal reprimand, he was able to return to practice within a year of his conviction.

There is a parallel here with relatives who help their loved ones to die in order to relieve their suffering, who are also very unlikely

[47] *R v Cox* (1992) 12 BMLR 38.

to be successfully prosecuted for murder. Even if a prosecution is initiated, as it was in the UK case of Kay Gilderdale, who helped her desperately ill daughter to die by injecting her with morphine, juries are generally reluctant to convict. So the absolute prohibition on euthanasia coexists with a criminal justice system that is capable of showing sympathy towards people who break the law in order to relieve the suffering of others, and which is capable of distinguishing between selfish and compassionate acts of killing. If this is possible at the level of prosecution and conviction, why not provide greater clarity and certainty by distinguishing between selfish and compassionate acts of euthanasia and assisted suicide at the level of the definition of the offence? If it is possible to tell after the event if leniency in prosecution or sentencing is justifiable, surely it would also be possible to set out, in advance, the factors which can, in certain limited circumstances, justify helping someone to die?

There is something else wrong with the argument that ending patients' lives is incompatible with the ethics of the medical profession. As we have seen, doctors in some clinical specialities routinely engage in practices that will lead to patients' deaths, like removing their feeding tubes or sedating them into a coma from which they will never recover. If ending a patient's life by allowing them to starve to death is acceptable, it seems disingenuous to suggest that achieving the same outcome in a quicker and less distressing way *must* be incompatible with basic principles of medical ethics, unless the act/omission distinction is capable of doing much more moral work than I believe it can.

In any event, legalised assisted dying does not need to involve *doctors* killing their patients. In Switzerland, Dignitas clinics are staffed by volunteers who are generally not doctors. While medical advice on fatal doses is necessary, mixing up the solution and handing it to the patient, and even helping them to drink it, are not tasks that have to be carried out by registered medical practitioners. Indeed until fairly recently, doctors in Switzerland were positively excluded from the final acts involved in assisted suicide, because being paid for their services could amount to a 'selfish' motive, and hence be against the law.

Giving drugs intravenously is also something that can be accomplished by a non-specialist, as people with diabetes and women undergoing IVF already know. And other non-invasive methods of assisted suicide are possible: oxygen deprivation through a breathing mask containing helium, for example, can be accomplished by a non-specialist, and is both quick and painless.

This leads to the possibility that, in the future, debates over 'physician-assisted suicide' will start to seem rather old-fashioned. It is easy to buy helium (it is readily and cheaply available for filling party balloons), and while an airtight 'tent' or mask is also necessary, these too are not difficult to obtain. Dr Philip Nitschke, an Australian pro-euthanasia campaigner, has broadcast a video showing how to 'cook' the barbiturate pentobarbital (brand name Nembutal), in a modified pressurised oven-top espresso jug. The process takes 6-8 hours, and uses ingredients which again can be purchased fairly easily.

While of course suicide has always been an option for patients who retain the physical capacity to end their lives, the most effective ways of killing oneself are often brutal and frightening, and additionally mean that someone else will have to find one's body. Simply overdosing on readily available medication may be simple, but it can lead to an agonising death, or to living on in an even more debilitated state.

If it instead becomes easy for patients to obtain the means to take their own lives painlessly and effectively, will we have an epidemic of self-accomplished suicide among the terminally ill? Obtaining lethal medication by following a 'recipe' or purchasing a helium 'tent' on the internet would offer no protection at all to the vulnerable, though it would mean that doctors would be absolved of involvement in and responsibility for their patients' self-induced deaths.

C. Regulatory Difficulties

A different sort of argument against legalisation arises from pessimism about our ability to construct a safe and effective assisted dying law. First, it is sometimes argued that it would be hard to ensure that requests were voluntary, competent and sufficiently well informed. Secondly, it is suggested that both drawing regulatory lines and policing them would be so difficult that we would end up sliding down a slippery slope and extending access to assisted dying to a much wider population than we originally intended. I shall deal with these points in turn.

i. *Ensuring Requests are Voluntary, Competent and Informed*

Obviously, if it were to be legalised, it would be of vital importance to ensure that patients' requests for assisted dying had been made voluntarily. For a number of reasons, it has been suggested that in practice this represents an insuperable obstacle to legalisation. First, euthanasia is generally requested by patients who are extremely ill, and whose judgement may be distorted by the depression which can accompany the final stages of terminal illness. Because it would be hard to *guarantee* that a patient's desire to die was genuine – and not, for example, a symptom of their treatable depression – it has been argued that we should be extremely reluctant to comply with any patient's request for euthanasia.

Secondly, because the consequence of euthanasia will be the patient's death, there is no scope for correcting decisions based upon assumptions which subsequently prove to be mistaken. It might, for example, emerge that the patient lacked capacity when they made the decision to die. Alternatively, they may have been wrongly diagnosed with a terminal and incurable illness. Or the decision to die may have been based upon a misunderstanding of what was likely to happen to them as their disease progressed. Given the finality of euthanasia and the risk of these sorts of errors, opponents of legalisation have argued that we could never be sufficiently certain that a person's request for euthanasia was competent, settled, informed and voluntary. Finally, because consultations between patients and their doctors are protected by the principle of patient confidentiality, in practice it might be difficult to exercise much control over doctors' oral discussions with their patients. The privacy of the doctor–patient relationship would, it has been argued, make it almost impossible to ensure that the patient had not been pressurised into requesting euthanasia.

Of course, the obvious response to all these arguments is that we already allow patients to make decisions which will result in their deaths when we respect their refusals of life-prolonging medical treatment. A patient who is connected to a mechanical ventilator may be depressed, and we may wrongly judge her to be competent, but this inescapable risk of error does not persuade us that we should not allow patients to refuse treatment which is necessary to prolong their life. The exceptionally grave consequences of a mistaken diagnosis of capacity when patients choose to refuse life-saving treatment do not offer sufficient grounds for overriding their right to refuse unwanted treatment. Instead the appropriate response is a careful assessment of the individual patient's decision-making capacity. Nor do we think that the principle of patient confidentiality represents an insurmountable obstacle to our ability to protect vulnerable patients from being coerced into agreeing to the withdrawal of life-prolonging treatment.

If we are concerned that patients might make hasty decisions to die, based upon partial or inadequate information about what lies ahead for them, this might be an argument for an enforced waiting period between a person's initial request for an assisted death and assistance actually being provided. The longer the waiting period, the more certain we could be that the person who has asked for an assisted death is not going to change their mind. Indeed, where the person's desire for death is prompted by a sudden change in their health status – from being healthy and active to finding themselves paralysed from the neck down, for example – it could be argued that they should be given the chance to adjust to their new paralysed state before it would be acceptable to help them end their life. A balance has to be struck between respecting the individual's wishes and ensuring that safeguards are in place to try to ensure that assisted death is strictly an option of last resort for patients whose desire to die is settled and unwavering.

In a related argument, it has been suggested that if euthanasia were readily available, elderly patients might be pressurised into opting for a premature death. While most people who care for their elderly and/or sick relatives do so selflessly and treat them with great respect, this is not universally the case. What is often referred to as 'elder abuse' is a significant social problem, and it should undoubtedly give us pause for thought when contemplating the legalisation of assisted dying. It would be critically important to ensure that a request for assisted dying was not the culmination of the patient's systematic mistreatment by someone close to them.

Moreover, pressure from relatives need not be direct. If someone is moved by their children into an unpleasant residential care home, where they feel lonely and isolated, they might decide that assisted dying would be preferable to eking out their days surrounded by strangers who patronise and mistreat them. Yet if they were helped to continue to live in their own home, close to their friends and the communities of which they are a part, their desire for assisted dying might disappear. This is why any law which legalised assisted dying would, in my view, need to have not only a 'palliative care filter', where other palliative options should be explored before assisted dying becomes an option, but also a 'social support filter', where it would be necessary to work out whether additional support, perhaps to enable them to continue to live in their own home, could help the person to gain value and meaning from their life.

In addition to the problem of abuse, it is also common for elderly people to perceive themselves to be a burden to their families, and if death were an option, there is a danger that they might request euthanasia despite their desire to go on living. Of course, we should ensure that the person genuinely wants to bring their life to an end, and that people are not opting for assisted dying just because they think it would be more convenient for others, but we should not necessarily discount the idea that being a burden can be a horrible experience. Someone might quite reasonably prefer that their daughter does not sacrifice her own life in order to tend to them during a long period of extreme dependence.

In addition, it is sometimes suggested that pressure to opt for an earlier death might come from the medical profession. Assisted death, it is argued, might be cheaper than providing optimum palliative care, and so could represent a particularly cost-effective 'treatment' for old age and terminal illness. Of course it would be unethical for a doctor to try to persuade her patients to choose euthanasia, but it has been argued that simply mentioning death as an option might subtly influence a patient's decision.

There are two objections to this. First, for doctors to enthusiastically engage in 'bumping off' their elderly patients in order to save money and unblock beds runs counter to everything we know about modern medicine and its approach to death. Death is increasingly regarded as a failure, and doctors are trained to do their utmost to save and prolong life. It is simply implausible that the legalisation of assisted dying would lead the medical profession to encourage their patients to die, and no one who makes this sort of claim has offered any evidence to substantiate it.

Secondly, this claim rests upon the assumption that a request for assisted death would simply be granted, making the only 'cost' involved that of preparing and delivering the lethal injection. My point, however, is that well-crafted assisted dying law would demand a great deal more than this. If it were to have an effective palliative and social care filter, as I argue it should, it would certainly not be a cheap option. In Belgium, a Euthanasia Act was passed at the same time as a statute protecting the right to palliative care, and public funding for palliative care services was doubled. Doing one's best to find other ways to alleviate the person's distress or fear of dying can be time-consuming and expensive, and allowing assisted death to be an option when other avenues have been exhausted does not suggest that we are abandoning people at the end of life because it is simpler and cheaper if they just die.

Again, if there is a risk that patients might opt for a course of action that will result in their death out of a sense of obligation, or as a result of more direct pressure, this must be equally or perhaps even more true when death is achieved by treatment withdrawal.

If we are concerned to protect vulnerable patients from electing a premature death against their wishes, we should probably be more concerned about refusals of life-prolonging treatment, where the patient's decision must be respected even if it is wholly irrational, than about legalised euthanasia, which would only be available in certain tightly circumscribed circumstances. The legalisation of assisted dying would not present a unique opportunity for the mistreatment of the elderly. Common practices, such as withholding or withdrawing life-prolonging treatment without the patient's consent, may pose an even greater risk to vulnerable individuals. As we have seen, Do Not Attempt Resuscitation orders are generally made without consulting the person whose life is at stake, and resort to terminal sedation is subject to no formal safeguards at all.

Evidence from countries that have legalised assisted dying does not suggest that the people who have used it have been especially vulnerable. In fact, the evidence appears to indicate that, as a group, they do *not* come from the most vulnerable sections of society. For example, it has been suggested that women – as a result of their greater longevity and cultural assumptions about their propensity for self-sacrifice – might be more likely than men to feel pressurised into requesting assisted suicide, perhaps in order to avoid being a burden to their adult children. Yet in Oregon in 2009, more men (52.5 per cent) than women (47.5 per cent) died as a result of assisted suicide. Also in Oregon, comparatively few very elderly people make use of assisted dying – in 2009, 86.3 per cent of the people who died were under the age of 85. The vast majority were white (98.3 per cent) and comparatively well educated (70.7 per cent had some college education). Most had enrolled in hospice care (91.5 per cent), and most had private health insurance (84.7 per cent).[48]

Insofar as the risk of abuse exists, it is not clear that this is best addressed by an absolute prohibition on euthanasia. On the contrary, when euthanasia is practised covertly, the risk of abuse will be magnified by the secrecy and lack of transparency that are the

---

[48] Oregon Department of Human Services (n 8).

inevitable consequence of illegality. In countries where assisted dying is illegal, doctors who help their patients to die risk prosecution and they are therefore very unlikely to seek a second opinion. If we believe that there is a possibility that pressure will be exerted on sick and elderly patients, a carefully regulated system might in fact offer much more effective protection than a blanket ban. An absolute prohibition may simply push the practice underground, thus ensuring that assisted dying will be unsafe and unethical.

ii. Slippery Slopes

It is common for opponents of legalisation to make the slippery slope claim that even if we were to accept that doctors might sometimes act reasonably when they comply with a patient's request for assisted dying, we should nevertheless prohibit it because sanctioning some compassionate acts of killing would make it very difficult to prevent patients' lives being ended more frequently than we had intended. Even if we were to start with the best of intentions, restricting access to assisted dying to a small and tightly circumscribed group of patients, proponents of slippery slope arguments maintain that we would, in practice, not be able to stop ourselves from sliding down the slope towards patently unethical practices. There are essentially three sorts of 'slopes' that are pointed to by opponents of legalisation: the logical slippery slope, the empirical slippery slope and the psychological slippery slope.

a. Logical Slippery Slopes

A logical slippery slope argument involves the claim that it would be impossible to find rational and defensible grounds for distinguishing between different cases, so that once we commit ourselves to allow assisted dying in one set of circumstances – perhaps for people who have made a settled, voluntary decision to die – we are logically committed to allowing it in another set of circumstances

– perhaps for anyone who is temporarily unhappy – because we will not be able to find any non-arbitrary reasons for treating these cases differently. Yet this is clearly absurd, since it suggests that there is no line to be drawn here at all. It would be like saying that once we accept that there is a defence to murder if someone puts a loaded gun to your head, we are committed to allowing a defence to murder if someone accidentally bumps into you on a crowded bus, or makes a derogatory remark about your new haircut.

A more subtle version of the logical slippery slope claim suggests that once we are committed to permitting euthanasia for competent patients who are suffering unbearably, we would have no grounds for confining it to those patients, and would be committed to permitting it for patients who lack capacity, or who are not suffering at all. This is a more complex and plausible claim, and it requires some unpicking. The argument runs something like this: if the justification for legalisation is compassion, it is impossible to confine assisted dying to people who are competent, because people who lack capacity may also be capable of suffering. If, on the other hand, the justification is autonomy, we don't have any reason to impose a requirement of unbearable suffering. If the person's autonomous request is, on its own, sufficient justification, then we are committed to allowing assisted dying for lovesick teenagers, whose distress may be very real indeed, but is overwhelmingly likely to be short-lived.

I deal with this argument in a little more depth below when considering what safeguards an assisted dying law might contain, but, in short, as a slippery slope claim it doesn't work because it treats these two justifications – suffering and autonomy – as if only one of them would be necessary in order to sanction assisting a patient's death. Instead, it would be possible for there to have to be both an autonomous choice *and* unbearable suffering before a doctor could legitimately help a patient to die. Given that assisted dying involves a third person bringing about a patient's death, it is not unreasonable to suggest that *both* unendurable suffering *and* an autonomous request should be necessary before a doctor is entitled to conclude that assisting a patient's death would be compatible with his legal duty of care towards his patient and his ethical responsibility to 'do no harm'.[49]

Of course it is true that doctors are sometimes entitled to treat a patient without his consent, as happens when someone lacks capacity to give a valid consent to treatment. But it would be possible for assisted dying to be a special case, which could be carried out only following a competent patient's explicit request. There is nothing about allowing assisted dying for competent suffering adults which necessarily commits us to allowing it for incompetent or non-suffering patients.

b. Empirical Slippery Slopes

An empirical slippery slope involves the claim that once we allow assisted dying in one case, there will be an irresistible slide towards allowing practices which we cannot defend in the same way. This is an empirical claim not about what we would be logically committed to if we took the first step on the slope, but simply about what would be likely to happen. The most common version of the empirical slippery slope claim is that legalising voluntary euthanasia will make involuntary euthanasia more common. In order to establish the truth or falsity of such a claim, we might consult statistics from countries which have legalised assisted dying, such as the Netherlands and the state of Oregon in the US. John Keown, for example, claims that an unacceptably high proportion of deaths in the Netherlands are examples of non-voluntary euthanasia (0.4 per cent in 2005),[50] and he argues that this therefore proves that 'the Dutch experience lends weighty support to the slippery slope argument'.[51] But of course this is only an example of a slippery slope at work if we have established that there is a causal link between the legalisation of euthanasia in

---

[49] T Beauchamp and J Childress, *Principles of Biomedical Ethics,* 6th edn (Oxford, Oxford University Press).

[50] J Keown, 'Euthanasia in the Netherlands: Sliding down the Slippery Slope' in J Keown (ed), *Euthanasia Examined* (Cambridge, Cambridge University Press, 1995) 261–96.

[51] ibid.

the Netherlands and the Dutch medical profession's (alleged) willingness to end patients' lives without prior request.

Can causation be proved here? In order to establish this, we would need to compare data from before and after legalisation, and demonstrate: (a) that there was more involuntary killing after rather than before legalisation, and (b) that this change was caused by the change in the law. It is by no means clear that the former is, in fact true, but in any event it is important to remember that establishing a correlation is not the same as proving causation. Let's imagine, for example, that high-quality epidemiological research indicates that light to moderate alcohol consumption during pregnancy correlates with *better* cognitive and behavioural outcomes for some babies.[52] Of course, as the authors of this study were quick to point out, correlation does not establish a causal link, and a much more likely explanation of this study's findings is that light to moderate alcohol consumption correlates with better socio-economic circumstances and that it is the healthier lifestyles of middle-class women which cause their babies to be born with fewer behavioural and cognitive difficulties.[53]

Proof that a bad practice happens in a country in which euthanasia has been legalised does not, without more, establish that it was legalisation which caused the bad practice. I may, for example, have proof that a *good* practice – high-quality palliative care provision, perhaps – exists in a country (like Belgium) where euthanasia has been legalised. I may even have statistics which show that the proportion of patients accessing palliative care services is much higher in Belgium (where euthanasia is legal) than it is in the UK (where euthanasia is illegal), *and* that it is much higher in Belgium now than it was before euthanasia was legalised. The twin facts that Belgium has legalised euthanasia and that palliative care provision has improved do not, however, establish a *causal link* between legalisation and improvements in palliative care.

[52] Y Kelly, A Sacker, R Gray et al, 'Light Drinking in Pregnancy, a Risk For Behavioural Problems and Cognitive Deficits at 3 Years of Age?' (2009) 38 *International Journal of Epidemiology* 129–40.

[53] C Gavaghan, '"You can't handle the truth"; Medical Paternalism and Prenatal Alcohol Use' (2009) 35 *Journal of Medical Ethics* 300–03.

So is there proof of a causal link between the legalisation of euthanasia in the Netherlands and an (alleged) increase in the proportion of deaths which result from doctors ending life without a specific patient request? Below I explain that it is not at all clear that there has been an increase in involuntary euthanasia in the Netherlands, but in any event the comparative data necessary to substantiate the claim that the Dutch have slid down the slippery slope simply do not exist. We do know, however, that non-voluntary euthanasia is at least as common in countries where euthanasia is illegal, as it is the Netherlands. An anonymous survey of 1918 Australian physicians found that the proportion of all Australian deaths that involved a medical end-of-life decision were:

- voluntary active euthanasia: 1.8 per cent (including physician-assisted suicide: 0.1 per cent);
- ending of patient's life without patient's concurrent explicit request: 3.5 per cent;
- withholding or withdrawing of potentially life-prolonging treatment: 28.6 per cent;
- alleviation of pain with opioids in doses large enough that there was a probable life-shortening effect: 30.9 per cent.[54]

If Australian doctors 'end life without an explicit request' *more* frequently (3.5 per cent of all deaths) than doctors in the Netherlands (0.4 per cent of all deaths), it is certainly not self-evident that the legalisation of euthanasia in the Netherlands has been responsible for a greater propensity to engage in non-voluntary euthanasia. If we were to use the flawed logic of drawing conclusions about causation from the presence of a correlation, it would be possible to draw on the Australian survey in order to argue that it is the prohibition of euthanasia which causes more incidences of ending life without a patient's explicit request. But that would be a mistake, because we simply do not have sufficient evidence to establish causation. Rather, all we can tell from

---

[54] H Kuhse, P Singer, P Baume, M Clark and M Rickard, 'End-of-Life Decisions in Australian Medical Practice' (1997) 166 *Medical Journal of Australia* 191.

comparative data on end-of-life decision-making is that the evidence that there are more cases of involuntary euthanasia in the Netherlands than there are in countries where euthanasia is illegal is weak, and the evidence that legalisation causes more cases of non-voluntary euthanasia is non-existent.

A comparative study of end-of-life decisions (including treatment withdrawal and giving doses of painkillers which could hasten death and euthanasia) was carried out in six European countries, at a time when euthanasia and assisted suicide could be practised openly only in the Netherlands.[55] Unsurprisingly, for both competent and incompetent patients, end-of-life decisions were discussed openly most frequently in the Netherlands. For competent patients in the Netherlands, the end-of-life decision was not discussed with the patient in 5 per cent of cases; in Italy the figure was 52 per cent and in Sweden 53 per cent. Where the patient was incompetent, the decision had not been discussed with the patient or relatives in 12 per cent of cases in the Netherlands, and 58 per cent in both Italy and Sweden. Shockingly, then, when Italian and Swedish doctors take steps that will result in a patient's death, in the majority of cases this is kept from both the patient herself and her relatives. In addition, in Italy, only 18 per cent of doctors consulted another doctor before making an end-of-life decision, and only 12 per cent consulted nursing staff. In contrast, in the Netherlands, 43 per cent discussed the decision with another doctor and 36 per cent discussed it with nursing staff.

A study of neonatal deaths found that *more* neonatal physicians in France (73 per cent) had administered drugs to neonates with the purpose of ending life than in the Netherlands (47 per cent).[56]

---

[55] A van der Heide, L Deliens, K Faisst, T Nilstun, M Norup, E Paci, G van der Wal and PJ van der Maas, 'End-of-Life Decision-Making in Six European Countries: Descriptive Study' (2003) 362 *The Lancet* 345–50.

[56] M Cuttini, M Nadai, M Kaminski, G Hansen, R de Leeuw, S Lenoir, J Persson, M Rebagliato, M Reid, U de Vonderweid, HG Lenard,M Orzalesi and R Saracci for the EURONIC Study Group, 'End-of-Life Decisions in Neonatal Intensive Care: Physicians' Self-Reported Practices in Seven European Countries' (2000) 355 *The Lancet* 2112–18.

If patients' lives are ended in the absence of an explicit request with similar or even greater frequency in countries which have *not* legalised euthanasia, it is far from clear that the evidence backs up the claim that the legalisation of euthanasia in the Netherlands has caused any propensity to engage in non-voluntary euthanasia.

In 2009, Judith Rietjens et al published a meta-analysis of all of the studies into euthanasia in the Netherlands that had been conducted in the previous two decades.[57] In 1990, shortly after the Dutch courts started carving out a defence of 'necessity' in cases where doctors had ended a patient's life, 1.7 per cent of all deaths were the result of euthanasia. This figure rose to 2.4 per cent in 1995, and again to 2.6 per cent in 2001, the year in which the relevant statute was formally amended to permit euthanasia. Importantly, however, in the study which followed the passing of assisted dying legislation, in 2005, the upward trend was in fact *reversed*, and the proportion of all deaths that were the result of euthanasia dropped back to 1.7 per cent.

One possible explanation for this reduction in deaths from euthanasia in the Netherlands is that, in recent years, the proportion of deaths attributable to terminal sedation has correspondingly increased. Some commentators have suggested that this may be because there is less 'red tape' associated with involvement in a death produced by terminal sedation. Yet terminal sedation is lawful in countries where euthanasia is not. Analysts of the Netherlands data who suggest that this is a worrying trend – with doctors avoiding the strictures of the reporting requirements by using terminal sedation instead – are making a rather interesting move, since the implication is that resort to a practice which is perfectly lawful, and *unregulated*, in countries like the US and the UK is more worrying than resort to heavily regulated euthanasia.

In addition to a reduction in the number of deaths through

---

[57] JAC Rietjens, PJ van der Maas, BD Onwuteaka-Philipsen, JJM van Delden, and A van der Heide, 'Two Decades of Research on Euthanasia from the Netherlands. What Have We Learnt and What Questions Remain?' (2009) 6 *Journal of Bioethical Inquiry* 271–83.

euthanasia in the Netherlands in recent years, there has also been a reduction in the number of euthanasia requests – from 9700 in 2001 to 8400 in 2005. Furthermore, the frequency of 'ending of life without an explicit patient request', which opponents of legalisation point to as evidence of the Dutch sliding down a slippery slope, has also decreased from 0.8 per cent of all deaths in 1990 to 0.4 per cent in 2005. Unless these figures are wildly inaccurate, this does not look like an uncontrollable slide down a slippery slope. Further analysis of these cases of 'ending of life without an explicit request' suggests that these are generally cases where patients are now incompetent, and close to death, and are given life-ending doses of opioids. This, as we have seen, would often also be lawful in countries where euthanasia is illegal, justified by the doctrine of double effect.

In the early days of legalised euthanasia in the Netherlands, there was substantial criticism of the reporting mechanisms, with many cases of euthanasia remaining unreported. But in recent years, the reporting rate in the Netherlands has also increased, from 18 per cent in 1990 to 80 per cent in 2005. While 80 per cent may still sound inadequate, the non-reported deaths are generally ones which some doctors believe are not, in fact, instances of euthanasia, because they involve giving opioids, in doses that could be justifiable under the doctrine of double effect. For deaths induced by neuro-muscular relaxants and barbiturates, where the doctrine of double effect has no purchase, the reporting rate is 99 per cent.[58]

c. Psychological Slippery Slopes

The third sort of slippery slope claim involves a *psychological* slippery slope, in which, over time, we become accustomed to the idea of assisted death and as it becomes routine and familiar, taking a further step down the slope becomes less alarming. An example might be that we gradually become used to the idea

---

[58]   ibid.

of assisted dying for the terminally ill, and after a while we feel more relaxed about allowing it for people whose conditions are not terminal, and once assisted dying for people with chronic conditions becomes 'normal', we are ready to contemplate euthanasia for those who are temporarily incapacitated, and so on. In short, this sort of claim is that over time we will become desensitised to the horror of killing, and be increasingly willing to expand the circumstances in which it is an acceptable response to suffering.

But is it really true that an acceptance that ending life can be legitimate in certain circumstances inevitably leads to the progressive expansion of those circumstances?

It is relatively common for opponents of euthanasia to suggest that relaxing the prohibition of euthanasia will lead to a 'general moral decline', and to point to Nazi Germany as the paradigm example of this.[59] We should, however, be cautious about claims of a downhill road to Nazi death camps. The Nazis subscribed to theories of race hygiene, exterminating those whom they judged to pose a threat to the genetic health of the nation, in part through the risk of interbreeding with people of Aryan stock.[60] Arthur Caplan goes so far as to argue that invoking the Holocaust analogy too readily 'diminishes the horror done by Nazi scientists and doctors to their victims'.[61] While the Nazis may have labelled some of their activities 'euthanasia', this was always a misnomer, because the motivation was never a compassionate response to individual suffering, and certainly wasn't intended to bring about a good or a gentle and easy death. Accepting that euthanasia and assisted suicide are sometimes understandable and justifiable responses to unbearable suffering does not commit us to a progressive expansion of what we mean by 'unbearable suffering', nor does it mean that we are inevitably set on a path that ends in

---

[59] D Giesen, 'Dilemmas at Life's End: A Comparative Legal Perspective' in J Keown (ed), *Euthanasia Examined* (Cambridge, Cambridge University Press, 1995) 204.

[60] AL Caplan, 'Misusing the Nazi Analogy' (2005) 309 *Science* 535.

[61] ibid.

the involuntary extermination of disabled people.

In relation to all three slippery slope arguments, it is clearly false that a blanket ban is the optimum response to concerns about a practice's potential misapplication. If we can imagine circumstances in which euthanasia or assisted suicide might be legitimate, prohibiting it completely in order to prevent it being employed in other less compelling situations is a peculiarly blunt approach to regulation, especially since the consequence for patients who do clearly merit access to euthanasia will be a protracted, painful or otherwise intolerable death. It would be more logical to advocate regulations confining access to euthanasia to patients whose circumstances lie towards the top of the slope, and prohibiting it in other cases. Obviously, it would be necessary to work out what factors justify allowing a doctor to actively cause a patient's death, and I do not mean to imply that either drawing or policing this boundary would be an easy task. The slippery slope claim is not that it would be *challenging* to regulate euthanasia effectively, but rather that it would be *impossible*. Without more persuasive evidence, hypothetical and pessimistic speculation about our inability to regulate euthanasia does not offer an adequate justification for a refusal to contemplate thinking about what effective regulation might involve.

V. WHAT MIGHT AN ASSISTED DYING LAW LOOK LIKE?

A. Other Countries' Experience

As mentioned earlier, a number of other countries have experience of legalised assisted dying. The most commonly cited example is the Netherlands, which gradually adapted its defence of 'necessity' – that is, having an irreconcilable conflict of duties – in the criminal law to cover cases in which a doctor was faced with a patient whose suffering could be alleviated only by causing their death. After 20 years of court decisions, a statute was passed which permits both voluntary euthanasia and assisted suicide (euthanasia is in practice much more common), provided the 'due care' criteria are met.[62] These are that the physician:

(a) holds the conviction that the request by the patient was voluntary and well-considered;

(b) holds the conviction that the patient's suffering was lasting and unbearable;

(c) has informed the patient about the situation he was in and about his prospects;

(d) and the patient hold the conviction that there was no other reasonable solution for the situation he was in;

(e) has consulted at least one other, independent physician who has seen the patient and has given his written opinion on the requirements of due care referred to in parts (a)–(d); and

(f) has terminated a life or assisted in a suicide with due care.

The doctor who carries out euthanasia must be the patient's own doctor – hence the Dutch have excluded the possibility of euthanasia 'tourism'.

In Belgium, there was no gradual development in case law, but instead the Belgian parliament passed a Euthanasia Act in 2002 which legalised only euthanasia. To be eligible, patients must be over the age of 18, competent and conscious, and their requests for euthanasia must be explicit, unambiguous, repeated, and durable. The patient must be in a hopeless situation, suffering from persistent and unbearable pain or distress that cannot be alleviated, and must be suffering from a serious and incurable disorder. In practice, following a patient's request for euthanasia, a palliative care nurse will spend time with her in order identify the reasons for her request.[63] Finding out why a patient wants their life to be brought to an end helps the nurse to work out what palliative response might be able to alleviate the suffering that underlies the patient's request for euthanasia. Once other palliative options have been explored, a second doctor must consult the patient's medical

---

[62] The Termination of Life on Request and Assisted Suicide (Review Procedures) Act 2001, s 2.

[63] B Dierckx de Casterlé et al, 'Nurses' Views on their Involvement in Euthanasia: A Qualitative Study in Flanders (Belgium)' (2006) 32 *Journal of Medical Ethics* 187–92.

file, examine the patient and confirm that the patient's suffering is unbearable, and that it cannot be alleviated. Compliance with these criteria is judged, after the event, by a national review committee.

Oregon, and now the state of Washington too, have legalised only assisted suicide, and this is not available to non-residents, in order to avoid these states becoming destinations for suicide tourism. The Oregon Death with Dignity Act 1994 provides that a physician may comply with a competent, terminally ill, adult patient's voluntary request for a prescription of drugs,which will allow her to end her life in a humane and dignified manner. The patient must make an initial oral request, followed by a formal written request. At least 15 days after the written request, the patient must repeat their request orally, and a further 48 hours must elapse before the prescription can be filled. The patient's request must be witnessed by two people other than the doctor, at least one of whom must not be a relative, an heir or an employee of the institution in which the patient is receiving care. The patient must be asked to notify her family. A second doctor must confirm the patient's diagnosis and that the patient is competent and acting voluntarily. The patient must have received complete information about her diagnosis, prognosis and alternative treatments, such as hospice care and pain control. If there is any suggestion that the patient is depressed or has a psychiatric disorder, she must be referred to a psychiatrist or psychologist.

As we saw earlier, assisting suicide is a criminal offence under the Swiss Penal Code only if the defendant's motive is 'selfish'. Thus, provided that a person's motive for assisting a suicide is compassionate, no offence is committed. A number of 'right to die' organisations offer assistance with suicide to their members. EXIT insists that patients must be over the age of 18, mentally competent, and suffering from intolerable health problems. EXIT will also only help Swiss nationals to commit suicide, while Dignitas allows foreigners to join and have access to assisted suicide in its Zurich clinic.

Each of these models is a product of the cultural and social context from which it emerged, and so it would be foolish to imagine that one could just transplant the Swiss model, say, to Australia or Canada. Nevertheless, there are two interesting points to note from other countries' experience with legalised assisted dying. First, it is critical to recognise the importance of the 'starting point' from which legalised assisted dying has developed. In the Netherlands and in Switzerland, there was not a sudden decision to change the law, rather there was a gradual development, or carving out, of existing provisions in the criminal codes. This may have advantages over immediate legalisation via a new statute. It might, for example, be easier to 'take people with you' if change is incremental. On the other hand, incremental change does not offer the same opportunity for open scrutiny and public debate.

Most discussions of the legalisation of assisted dying tend to take for granted that change will be both sudden and comprehensive, generally as a result of a statute which, when it becomes law, creates a new defence to the crimes of murder and/or assisted suicide. But it is important to acknowledge that legal change can also take place over time, as it did in the Netherlands. One way in which this might happen in a country like the UK might be to argue that terminal sedation, discussed earlier, as well as being a solution to extreme distress in an emergency, might also be a treatment which a competent patient should be able to request, in advance. Access to continuous deep sedation until death, upon request, would be very like access to euthanasia, but it would be a smaller step than a new Assisted Dying Act.

Secondly, in all of the countries where euthanasia or assisted suicide is lawful, there is some prospective scrutiny of decisions to allow a patient to have an assisted death, often involving the need for a second opinion, *and* some retrospective investigation of whether the decision was compatible with the rules. In the Netherlands, for example, each case of euthanasia or assisted suicide is considered by a regional review committee, usually consisting of a lawyer, a doctor and an ethicist. If the committee is satisfied that the criteria have been fulfilled, the case is closed without informing the public prosecutor, who is notified only if the committee finds that the doctor did not fulfil the due care criteria. In about 6 per cent of cases each year, the regional review committee asks for more information, usually for further evidence that the patient's suffering was unbearable. In a handful of cases each year, it makes a finding of non-compliance with the 'due care' criteria (0.6 per cent in 2007).[64] Prosecution is then possible.

Different weight is given to prospective authorisation and retrospective investigation in different legal systems, but it would be reasonable to conclude that both might be advisable. Where a decision will result in death, it would be inappropriate to allow the doctor to go ahead without *some* additional safeguard, like a second opinion, and there would have to at least be the possibility of an investigation, after the event, so that cases which did not fall within the rules can be identified and prosecuted.

B. Process

Leading on from this, it is important to recognise that permitting legalised assisted dying would not necessarily mean replacing the criminal prohibition of euthanasia and assisted suicide with something much more permissive. Rather, euthanasia and assisted suicide should continue to be criminal offences, but defences might exist if a set of criteria are met. In Switzerland, for example, the police are contacted immediately after any assisted suicide, and the circumstances are fully investigated in order to find out whether the assistance was lawful, in which case the case will be closed, or unlawful, in which case it is referred to the public prosecutor.

In relation to both euthanasia and assisted suicide, the choice is not necessarily between legality and illegality, rather it would also be possible for them to be regarded as *lesser* offences in certain

[64] Ministry of Health, Welfare and Sport, *Evaluation Termination of Life on Request and Assisted Suicide (Review Procedures) Act* (2007), available at www.minvws.nl/en/themes/euthanasia/default.asp.

circumstances. In Colombia, for example, there is a specific offence of 'mercy killing', when someone 'kills another person out of compassion, to put an end to intense suffering caused by physical injuries or grave or incurable illness', for which the punishment is imprisonment of six months to three years.[65] The Constitutional Court has further decided that medical professionals who carry out such an act with the consent of a terminally ill patient should have a complete defence.

There are two ways in which we could create defences for mercy killing and assisted suicide. The first would be akin to the defence of self-defence to a murder charge. Someone could help a patient die, and *after the event,* would be able to claim that they have a defence, and are not guilty. This would have the merit of simplicity and speed. Someone who is suffering unbearably could be killed by their doctor or helped to die by their partner, and we would rely on the good sense of prosecutors, judges and juries to determine whether, in the circumstances that existed at the time of the killing or the assisted suicide, the defence existed and prosecution, conviction or imprisonment is therefore unwarranted. We would not then need to devise a complex algorithm, capable of capturing all the factors which would need to be present, or absent, for an assisted suicide or an act of euthanasia to be sanctioned in advance. It would also avoid the need for cumbersome procedures through which decisions are made to prospectively sanction an assisted suicide or an act of euthanasia.

There are, however, substantial downsides to this case-by-case approach to assisted dying. It would not provide the 'insurance policy' or 'comfort blanket' that legalised assisted dying offers to people with degenerative diseases. They would know that someone could assist them to die when the time comes, but that person would have to run the risk of prosecution, and for many dying people, this is too much to ask of relatives whom they already know will suffer greatly in the aftermath of their death. Certainly doctors would rightly be unwilling to openly expose

---

[65] S Michalowski, 'Legalising Active Voluntary Euthanasia through the Courts: Some Lessons from Colombia' (2009) 17 *Medical Law Review* 183–218.

themselves to the risk of imprisonment in the hope that, after the event, the public prosecutor will exercise his prosecutorial discretion in their favour. If the medical profession is to be involved in helping patients to die, it would be reasonable for it to expect some prospective certainty about when euthanasia or assisted suicide is a crime, and when it is not.

It could also be argued that if we know *after the event* when an act of assisted suicide or euthanasia is acceptable, there is no reason why we can't attempt to describe *prospectively* what circumstances justify helping someone to die. A basic principle of the rule of law is that citizens are entitled to know, in advance, what the law is, so that they can take steps to ensure compliance. A system which required people to break the law, in the hope that they will be able to escape punishment, would fail to give citizens the certainty to which they are entitled about what is and what is not regarded as a serious crime. Indeed this could also be said to be a defect of the status quo in many countries where euthanasia and assisted suicide are serious criminal offences, but prosecution and convictions are unusual, to say the least.

A second way in which a defence could be created is by setting out in a statute what criteria have to be present for a statutory defence to exist. In the UK, a model for this exists in relation to abortion. Abortion in the UK is still a criminal offence under the Offences Against the Person Act 1861, but the Abortion Act 1967 provides that no offence will have been committed if the various requirements in the Act are followed – for example, that two doctors agree that one of the statutory grounds for abortion is satisfied, and that the pregnancy is terminated by a registered medical practitioner in an NHS hospital or approved place. In relation to assisted suicide and euthanasia, a similar model could be used. Both would continue to be criminal offences but a statute would specify when, if certain factors are present and if certain procedures are followed, no offence will have been committed. This would require us to set out, in advance, what substantive factors should be present and what processes should be followed to turn these crimes into lawful behaviour. I shall consider what these might be below.

As mentioned earlier, there would also need to be some mechanism through which cases in which the rules were not followed could be identified, with the possibility of prosecution if appropriate. Prospective authorisation could not amount to a licence to kill, without rigorous processes in place to ensure that the rules are followed in practice, and that where the rules are broken, this is both identified and reported to the public prosecutor.

In the UK, there is currently a curious middle ground in relation to assisted suicide. It is a criminal offence, but prosecution can go ahead only with the consent of the Director of Public Prosecutions. In 2009, in *R (on the application of Purdy) v DPP*, the House of Lords found that – although the DPP could not give prospective immunity from prosecution to someone who intends to take a loved one to Switzerland – people are entitled to know what factors the DPP takes into account when deciding, after the event, whether prosecution is in the public interest.[66]

Following this judgment, the DPP set out the factors which count in favour of prosecution and the factors which count against.[67] There are 16 public interest factors in favour of prosecution, such as that the victim lacked capacity, or that he had not reached a voluntary, clear, settled and informed decision to commit suicide, and six public interest factors against prosecution, the most important of which is that 'the suspect was wholly motivated by compassion'. It is noteworthy that a factor in *favour* of prosecution is that 'the suspect was acting in his or her capacity as a medical doctor, nurse, other healthcare professional'. This has two consequences. First, it has led to concern among doctors that providing a patient with a copy of her medical notes to take to Switzerland could lead to prosecution for assisting her suicide. Secondly, since this policy applies to assisted suicide in general, and not only to those who accompany their relatives to Switzerland, at first sight it seems odd that the DPP might look more kindly on

---

[66] *R (on the application of Purdy) v DPP* [2009] UKHL 45.
[67] DPP, 'Policy for Prosecutors in Respect of Cases of Encouraging or Assisting Suicide', www.cps.gov.uk/publications/prosecution/assisted_suicide_policy.html.

someone who is more likely to bungle the attempt to help someone to take their own life, than on someone who can achieve this
end more speedily and effectively. But of course, the factors are
not binding statutory requirements, and each case is considered on
its merits.

In the first case decided under the new policy – that of
Caractacus Downes, who accompanied his parents Sir Edward
and Lady Downes to Zurich to die together – some of the factors
in favour of prosecution were present. For example, Sir Edward
and Lady Downes themselves would have been able to do some
of the acts that their son undertook on their behalf. But because
he was solely motivated by compassion, the DPP's conclusion
was that 'the public interest factors tending against prosecution
outweigh those tending in favour'.

This DPP's policy is clearly not legalisation of assisted suicide,
but it is official guidance as to when prosecution for assisting a
suicide would be inappropriate. This means that people in the UK
can assist a relative's suicide, having looked at the checklist in
advance to see whether they are likely to face prosecution, but
they cannot know for certain whether they might face up to 14
years in prison until after a police investigation and the DPP's
decision not to prosecute. So, while people who assist suicides by
taking their relatives to Switzerland are likely to avoid punishment, they cannot avoid running the risk of prosecution and
imprisonment.

C. Method: Assisted Suicide or Euthanasia, or Both?

If assisted dying were to be legalised, or partially decriminalised,
it would be necessary to decide whether the defence should apply
to assisted suicide and/or euthanasia. In assisted suicide, the final
act is committed by the patient, and legalisation would simply
allow someone else to help him. If only *physician*-assisted suicide
is legalised, then only doctors would be allowed to help patients
to die. Euthanasia would involve a third party, most likely a doc-

tor, injecting the patient with drugs that would kill him.

So which method is preferable? Some maintain that assisted suicide is preferable, partly because it helps us to be sure this is what the patient wants, and that they haven't changed their mind. A person could be prescribed lethal medication, but until the very last minute they can decide not to use it. Assisted suicide might also be easier for doctors, who are not asked to actively kill their patients.

On the other hand, there are compelling reasons for preferring euthanasia. Doctors can end patients' lives more quickly and effectively than the patients themselves, who might, for example, fail to ingest all of the prescribed dose and be left both alive and severely damaged by partially digesting the medication. Indeed, it is noteworthy, but not surprising, that a study in the Netherlands found that complications, such as vomiting, and problems with completion, such as a failure to induce coma, were much more common in cases of assisted suicide than they were when doctors performed euthanasia.[68] In 18 per cent of cases where the intention was that the doctor would assist the patient's suicide, the doctor in fact decided to administer the lethal medication himself. This conversion of assisted suicides into cases of euthanasia was most common when the patients were unable to take all of the medication themselves.

If assisted suicide is more likely to go wrong, preferring it to euthanasia is justifiable only if there is some residual fear that doctors might not be acting in accordance with the patient's wishes. In the states of Oregon and Washington, the prevailing view is that assisted suicide is preferable to euthanasia because it provides an additional safeguard. In his evidence to the House of Lords Select Committee which examined this issue in 2005, Dr Nick Gideonse, a general practitioner in Oregon, claimed that 'The fact that the patient self-administers in a way that is not easy

---

[68] JH Groenewoud, A van der Heide, BD Onwuteaka-Philipsen, DL Willems, PJ van der Maas and G van der Wal, 'Clinical Problems with the Performance of Euthanasia and Physician-Assisted Suicide in the Netherlands' (2002) 342 *New England Journal of Medicine* 551–56.

to do, drinking ounces of a bitter liquid, provides a final piece of clear evidence that this is completely volitional and self-administered'.[69] In her evidence, Barbara Coombs Lee told the Committee that 'having that last firewall, if you will, of having very clear self-administration, in this society, in this state, at this time is important to people, to have that reassurance that it really is a volitional act that a patient must take'.[70]

Against this, it might be argued that it is cruel and inhumane to require the patient's final act to be one that is not only unpleasant, but also difficult and stressful. An assisted death should be peaceful and comfortable, and this may be best facilitated by euthanasia rather than assisted suicide.

In addition, both an advantage and disadvantage of assisted suicide is that people who are fearful of the death that lies ahead of them might be able to obtain a prescription that they do not necessarily use. The advantage of this is that they can live their life to the full for as long as possible, with the reassuring knowledge that they have the means to end it if their suffering becomes unbearable. The prescription operates as a kind of 'comfort blanket', and might then serve to prolong rather than to shorten life.

There are, however, dangers is permitting people to obtain lethal medication without using it. Not only might it fall into the wrong hands, but also it means that someone who obtains the lethal prescription as an 'insurance policy against future suffering', but who then sinks into what might be a temporary depressive episode, has the means to end their life quickly and easily, when without ready access to lethal medication, they might otherwise seek medical help and receive effective treatment for their depression. This problem is not insurmountable, however. It would be possible for a patient to obtain a preliminary authorisation of their request for a lethal prescription, but with the need for further assessment before the medication is actually issued, to ensure that their circumstances, at that point, justify access to

---

[69] Select Committee on the Assisted Dying for the Terminally Ill Bill, n 45 above, 14

[70] ibid, 146

assisted suicide. And if the medication is not used within a set period of time, it would be possible for it to have to be returned to the dispensing pharmacist.

D. Substance

In addition to having to decide upon a procedural framework, one of the most contentious aspects of legalisation would be deciding what factors justify permitting someone to be helped to die. Should there be a competency requirement? Should assisted dying only be available to the terminally ill? If so, how should 'terminal' be defined? If there is an 'intolerable suffering' requirement, is the patient's subjective view of their suffering sufficient? Should assisted dying be available to people who are simply 'tired of life'?

It would, at the outset, be important that rules designed to protect patients do not, through repeated use, turn into a set of obstacles to be overcome by doctors. An imperfect analogy might be the requirement to obtain a person's informed consent before they undergo medical treatment or take part in a clinical trial. This is a legal prerequisite for treatment or research participation, but there is a danger that 'consenting' the patient/research participant is regarded as a time-consuming bureaucratic hurdle, before the important business of treatment or research can begin. Consent is treated as a one-off formality, rather than as an important and ongoing duty to provide the patient/research participant with whatever information they need in order to ensure that their consent to treatment or to take part in the trial continues to be informed and voluntary throughout.

The fear that, over time, the safeguards set out in an assisted dying law would come to be regarded in the same way as tiresome paperwork is an important concern, but it is not an insuperable one. Waiting periods, information provision, second opinions, psychiatric assessments and consultations with palliative and social support experts would be much more demanding than the provision of an information sheet and the need for the patient's signature on a consent form. A request for assisted dying should prompt thorough investigation of the person's circumstances, and this should be sufficiently challenging that it could not be reduced to some meaningless bureaucratic hurdle.

A different sort of concern is that if the person who decides whether a patient's circumstances warrant access to assisted dying is their doctor, patients could just 'shop around' until they find a doctor who interprets the statutory rules particularly loosely. If the criteria are to offer meaningful safeguards, there would need to be some way to ensure consistency of application. This could take the form of some centralised route for the prospective authorisation of access to assisted death, and nationwide retrospective monitoring of all assisted deaths, with prosecutions where the statutory criteria were not, in fact, met.

To eliminate the 'shopping around' problem, it would be possible, as in the Netherlands, for the only 'gatekeeper' to be the family doctor. This would probably not work as effectively in the UK or the US, however, where general practitioners have a rather different role from Dutch family doctors, who spend about half of each working day making home visits and who get to know their patients and their families especially well. The populations in the US and the UK, particularly in some urban areas, are extremely mobile, and less likely to have a long-standing relationship with a family doctor. In addition, in order to accommodate doctors' conscientious objections, there would have to be some alternative to the family doctor as gatekeeper.

Another issue which would have to be addressed is whether it might be appropriate to involve a person's family and carers in the decision to permit an assisted death. On the one hand, not all families are harmonious, and patient confidentiality would seem to rule out informing family members of a person's decision against their wishes. On the other hand, it is those close to the person who has expressed an interest in assisted dying who may be in the best position to offer the kind of support and love which could help to alleviate their psychosocial suffering.

Watching someone you care about suffer is a miserable experience, and whether the person's life ends as a result of assisted or natural death, the emotional burden of dying is – while principally that of the person who dies – unquestionably also shared by those close to them. Of course we should be worried about the abuse of sick and elderly people, but most families are not like this, and most people would do anything they can to alleviate the suffering of someone they love. Perhaps doctors should simply try to persuade anyone who requests an assisted death to involve their family in discussions both about their reasons for wanting to die, and about whether other care and support services might be able to alleviate their feelings of hopelessness.

It would also be of critical importance to distinguish between a desire to die, which is a symptom of depression and which might disappear if the depression is effectively treated, and a desire to die which is not transient, but instead permanent and irrevocable. It may not always be easy to tell the difference between temporary suicidal feelings, and an irrevocable desire to end one's suffering through an assisted death. Any assisted dying law would therefore need to include some sort of psychiatric assessment of the patient, so that requests prompted by short-lived or treatable mental anguish could be filtered out.

Just because someone has cancer, for example, psychiatrists and doctors should not assume that their desire to die is necessarily irrevocable. People with cancer can also suffer from treatable depression, and it is of crucial importance that this possibility is properly investigated and discounted before a doctor agrees that the person's suffering is unbearable and untreatable, and their desire to die permanent.

In addition, it is important to remember that doctors would not be entitled to act only on the grounds of the patient's *own* assessment that their suffering is unbearable. On the contrary, a doctor would only be complying with his legal and ethical duties as a doctor if he agreed with the patient that there is nothing that could be done to alleviate their suffering, other than to bring their life to an end.

Of course, one problem here would be that doctors and

patients may have different conceptions of suffering. Physicians tend to place more emphasis upon physical suffering, and less on dependency and the emotional toll of bodily deterioration. Patients' experiences of suffering are also variable and highly individualised. Indeed this may be one of the reasons why palliative care specialists often believe that they can relieve all suffering at the end of life – relying upon a fairly objective measure of what patients in the final stages of cancer generally need in order to be made comfortable – while many patients do not share the view that their own suffering, which only they can truly understand, can be adequately managed. The nature and extent of a person's suffering is simply not reducible to the nature and extent of their disease.

Some people have suggested that if the justification for assisted dying is autonomy, and the patient's own view of whether their life is worth living, there could be no grounds for restricting assisted dying to people whose doctors agree they are suffering unbearably. According to this objection to legalisation, there are no grounds for restricting access to people whose condition and suffering are, objectively speaking, extremely grave. If the justification for legalisation were simply patient autonomy, the fit and the healthy should have just as much right to an assisted death as a person in the final stages of motor neurone disease. But this would be to ignore the ethical responsibility, not to mention the legal duty not to commit a crime, of the person who does the assisting. We cannot stop a healthy, able-bodied person from committing suicide, but we would not have a defence to the criminal offence of assisting suicide if we positively helped them to do so. A defence should only exist in certain limited circumstances, where helping someone to die is defensible as a compassionate response to suffering which cannot be alleviated in any other way.

Given that assisted death involves implicating a third party in bringing a person's life to an end, there could never be a 'right' to such assistance. The right would be to ask for assistance from a willing doctor, or other third party, who would act appropriately only in certain limited circumstances, when helping someone to die could properly be said to be an act of responsible benevolence or compassion.

As I have said before, I am not in favour of killing and assisted suicide. Both should, in my view, remain serious criminal offences. Rather, I am arguing that *in certain circumstances*, there should be a defence because, *in certain limited circumstances*, it would be consistent with a doctor's ethical duty to alleviate suffering to help a patient to die. But it would patently *not* be consistent with a doctor's ethical responsibility to 'do no harm' for her to help a lovesick teenager to end his life. Doctors are not their patients' handservants, and in addition to taking the patient's views into account, they must also consider any treatment they offer to be consistent with their basic ethical duties of beneficence (doing good) and non-maleficence (doing no harm).[71] In almost all cases, helping to end a patient's life would patently be to 'do harm', and so legalising assisted dying would be to carve out a limited exception to this, based upon the recognition – which is already given substance by the doctrine of double effect and the rules governing treatment withdrawal – that sometimes hastening or causing death can be compatible with a doctor's duty of care towards his patients.

A further difficult question which we would have to address when designing an assisted dying law is whether it should be possible to draw up an advance directive, or 'living will', specifying that one wants to have one's life brought to an end in the future, after one has lost capacity. One compelling argument against this possibility might be that someone cannot know what it would be like to be profoundly incapacitated, and holding them to a decision to opt for assisted death when they might find themselves to be a contented demented person, for example, would be problematic. More importantly still, if advance euthanasia directives were allowed, it would be necessary for someone other than the patient herself to determine the moment of her death, by decid-

---

[71] Beauchamp and Childress (n 49).

ing exactly when to implement the patient's living will.

It could be that these considerations present insuperable obstacles to the legalisation of euthanasia 'living wills'. If we have to be certain that assisted dying remains the person's considered preference at the moment at which it is carried out, rather than some months previously, it may be impossible to satisfy this condition when the person is no longer able to express a view. Assisted dying as a legitimate 'last resort' palliative option should involve discussions with the patient about their suffering and what other options might be able to alleviate it, and yet a binding euthanasia 'living will' might preclude such discussions. In addition, in so far as the critical justification for assisted dying is so that the person themselves can determine the moment of their death, it will seldom be possible to specify in advance, with sufficient precision, exactly when one wants to die.

On the other hand, if assistance with death is confined to the presently competent, there is a danger that someone might access it before they in fact want to die, fearing that they might otherwise lose capacity and become ineligible. There is also the danger that an assisted dying law which confines help to people who meet some competency threshold fails to help some people whose suffering is irremediable and unendurable. If the justification for assisted dying is compassion, then it would seem odd to be compassionate only towards those who happen to have mental capacity.

In short, in arguing in favour of legalisation we have to address the question of whether we are limiting access – to adults, to the terminally ill, to people who have mental capacity etc – because this is the only sort of law that is politically feasible? Or do we genuinely believe that these are the only circumstances in which assisted dying is legitimate?

My response to this objection is a mixed one. I would want to separate out restrictions which I believe are important in order to protect the vulnerable – the presence of unrelievable suffering and a palliative care and social support filter, for example. A palliative support filter would mean that a request for assisted dying would prompt thorough investigation of the person's reasons for seeking an assisted death. There will often be much that can be done to alleviate suffering, and it is critical that we weed out requests for assisted dying which are the product of inadequate access to palliative care, so that only requests which persist despite access to high-quality care are granted. A social support filter would involve trying to work out if there are other measures that could be taken to improve a person's quality of life, perhaps by enabling them to live in their own home and continue to be part of their social and community networks. The request for an assisted death would then represent the first step on a path towards a comprehensive evaluation of all that could be done to enable the person to continue to live as comfortably as possible. Assisted dying would then be a last resort, which would be justifiable only when it is clear that optimum care and support cannot relieve the person's suffering and obviate their desire for death.

Other restrictions on access to assisted dying may not be necessary in order to protect the vulnerable, but have sometimes been thought to be politically expedient. Terminal illness, in particular, is an odd and unjustifiable restriction. Doctors' predictions of life-expectancy are insufficiently accurate for 'having less than six months to live' to operate as a clear and fair boundary between those who should and those who should not have access to assisted dying. In addition to a lack of clarity, unbearable and irremediable suffering is not confined to those who are imminently dying, and if compassion is our justification for legalisation, it is that sort of suffering which should be the criterion, not terminal illness, especially since someone with longer to live will experience *more* suffering, quantitatively speaking, than someone whose death is expected within days. Of course, someone who is terminally ill may indeed be experiencing intolerable suffering with no possibility of alleviation, but we should not use 'terminal illness' as a convenient shorthand for what is really at stake: horrible suffering that cannot be alleviated in any other way.

VI. WHAT ARE THE CONSEQUENCES OF NOT TRYING?

Modern medicine cannot prolong life for ever: we will all die, and our experiences of dying will vary. When someone who has lived a full and happy life dies suddenly, in their sleep, at the age of 90, it may be very sad for the people who loved them that they are no longer alive, but it will be a relief that they did not suffer. Not all of us will be that fortunate, however, and for many people, the experience of dying is prolonged and miserable. Cancer can quite literally consume a person's body from the inside. Motor neurone disease may lead a person's bodily functions to deteriorate until they cannot breathe, speak or move, while their brain remains as sharp and lucid as ever.

Palliative care and the hospice movement have made the process of dying less institutionalised and more comfortable for millions of people. Every patient should have access to high-quality palliative and hospice care. But while many people's pain and distress can be effectively managed and alleviated, this is not universally the case. This is, of course, an empirical claim, but the evidence to support it is overwhelming. We know that the desire for the option of an assisted death exists among people who have access to good-quality palliative care. I started this essay with the reasons why Robert Baxter, Reg Crew and Tony Nicklinson, none of whom lacked good medical care, had sought assisted death. In the UK, Debbie Purdy has devoted years of her life to fighting a protracted battle in the courts in order to try to protect her husband from prosecution if he takes her to Switzerland in the future. She does not lack access to high-quality care, and yet she believes passionately that palliative care may not be able to prevent all of the suffering which she knows may lie ahead for her.

If it is true that palliative care cannot alleviate everyone's suffering, those who argue against the legalisation of assisted dying are forcing people like Reg Crew, Debbie Purdy, Tony Nicklinson and Robert Baxter to experience deaths that they don't want, because other people's values are more important than their own perception of their own suffering. Many opponents of legalisation argue that to permit assisted death would be to devalue the sick, the elderly and the dying, but this is illogical. Debbie Purdy is clear that there may come a time when she has had enough and wants to be helped to die, but this doesn't mean that, when that time comes, she will cease to be a valuable human being.

Opponents of assisted dying do have the right to say: 'This is not for me. I want to live until the bitter end, and, if I am a doctor, I want no part in helping patients to die.' They do not have the right to impose that preference on others.

Against Decriminalising Euthanasia; For Improving Care

John Keown

———⊸•⊱———

I. INTRODUCTION

S HOULD THE law allow doctors intentionally to kill their patients? When the euphemisms of 'doctor-assisted death' and 'assisted dying' are stripped away, this is the stark question at the heart of the euthanasia debate. The debate is not about whether doctors should be allowed to 'help people die'. That is what good doctors do, and have always done, by their skilful use of palliative medicine. It is what good nurses do, and have always done, by their dedicated care of dying patients. The euthanasia debate is not about killing pain; it is about killing patients. It has always been against our law and against professional medical and nursing ethics intentionally to kill patients or intentionally to help patients kill themselves. So, I will contend, it should remain.

I welcome the opportunity to deploy the case in favour of the current law and professional ethics. While the case for decriminalisation is repeatedly aired by a predominantly partisan mass media, the case against often struggles to get a fair hearing. Moreover, my opponent in this debate, Professor Emily Jackson, is a leading academic proponent of euthanasia. If, as I hope to show, the arguments she and others advance are unpersuasive, it will not be for want of an informed and enthusiastic advocate. Under our rules of engagement she and I have written our contributions blind, so I have not seen which arguments she has chosen to deploy. I shall, therefore, after a short introduction (section I) and a word about definitions (section II) reply (in section III) to a range of arguments, 10 in all, which are typically advanced in favour of decriminalisation. To give the reader a better sense of the debate as it has recently unfolded in the UK, I shall then (in section IV) evaluate the significant contribution to that debate made by Professor Jackson in the form of two articles and a book chapter,[1] and (in section V) briefly analyse Lord Joffe's Assisted Dying for the Terminally Ill Bill, which was considered by the House of Lords in 2006. Finally, I shall (in section VI) offer some brief conclusions.

The title of this book is *Debating Euthanasia*. The debate is not new: it has rumbled on in the UK and the US for decades. In recent years, however, the tactics of euthanasia campaigners have switched. Whereas they used to agitate for the decriminalisation of voluntary, active euthanasia (VAE) they now tend to limit their demands to 'physician-assisted suicide' (PAS). The 'Voluntary Euthanasia Society' has accordingly rebranded itself 'Dignity in Dying'. To respond to this change of tactics, I have widened my brief to rebut those who campaign solely for PAS and I shall therefore refer throughout to 'VAE/PAS': 'voluntary, active euthanasia and/or physician-assisted suicide'. As I will argue, the attempt to distinguish PAS from VAE fails: they are joined at the hip.

---

[1] E Jackson, 'Whose Death is it Anyway?: Euthanasia and the Medical Profession' (2004) 57 *Current Legal Problems* 415; E Jackson, 'Secularism, Sanctity and the Wrongness of Killing' (2008) 3 *Biosocieties* 125; E Jackson, 'Death, Euthanasia and the Medical Profession' in B Brooks-Gordon et al (eds), *Death Rites and Rights* (Oxford, Hart Publishing, 2007) 37. For reasons of space, and because her book chapter overlaps significantly with her first article, my focus will be her two articles. I shall post a reply on my webpage to Professor Jackson's contribution to *Debating Euthanasia* after I have read it: http://kennedyinstitute.georgetown.edu/ourpeople/keown.cfm.

If opinion polls are to be believed, the majority of people reading this book may well support VAE/PAS. That would not be surprising. The case for reform, with its slogans of 'the right to choose' and 'dying with dignity', has an obvious allure, particularly in secular, pluralistic societies. And who could fail to be moved by the plight of those (like Dianne Pretty) with motor neurone disease or (like Debbie Purdy) with multiple sclerosis who have spearheaded the media campaign for relaxation of the law? Don't we have a duty, in compassion, to 'help them die'? And aren't many doctors 'doing it' anyway, when they administer palliative drugs or switch off life-support machines at the patient's request, foreseeing that the patient's death will be hastened?

Some people who support VAE/PAS do so because they have seen loved ones die in distress, or because of their own fears about dying in distress. This is entirely understandable. There are urgent, grave questions about the limited availability of quality end-of-life care and about the 'medicalisation' of dying. Death and dying, once part of the fabric of everyday life, are now largely confined to institutions, and have become much less familiar to many of us. Many people fear that they will die in pain or will have their dying prolonged by 'meddlesome medicine'. We must, however, be careful before jumping to the conclusion that the answer to deficiencies in end-of-life care, including both under-treatment and over-treatment, is VAE/PAS. Whether the law should accommodate euthanasia is a question which calls for careful reflection, not misguided emotion, simplistic slogans or media sound-bites. We are debating changing the law for the whole of society, not just the ethics of individual cases. Very hard cases can indeed make very bad law. We are fortunate that few issues have been the subject of more comprehensive and informed expert debate. The case for VAE/PAS has been repeatedly aired and, with few exceptions, roundly rejected by legislatures and expert bodies worldwide, not least by the House of Lords, which has debated the matter across three-quarters of a century. Only last year it was rejected after careful consideration by the Scottish Parliament. This repeated rejection should give supporters of decriminalisation pause, especially if they have not consulted those legislative debates and expert reports. If the case for VAE/PAS is so strong, why has it repeatedly failed to persuade expert bodies which have examined it?

My contribution to this book will add its voice to the international chorus of rejection by making three central points. First, that decriminalising VAE/PAS would be wrong in principle. It would breach a basic human right: the 'right to life', the right not to be intentionally killed. Second, that the case for euthanasia on request is also, logically, a case for euthanasia without request. Professor Jackson's previous publications will help me make this point, for they openly support both. Third, that even if VAE/PAS were not wrong in principle in certain 'hard cases' (as when requested by a competent, suffering, terminally-ill patient), decriminalisation would pose grave risks to the vulnerable, especially the dying, the disabled and the disadvantaged. In particular, it would expose the competent but vulnerable to pressure to request an earlier death, and the incompetent to death without request.

II. DEFINITIONS

For the purpose of rebutting the current campaign for VAE/PAS I am content to adopt the definitions of 'euthanasia' and 'physician-assisted suicide' employed by the House of Lords Select Committee on Medical Ethics, chaired by Lord Walton, which reported in 1994. The Walton Committee defined 'PAS' as the provision of help by a doctor to a competent patient who had formed a desire to end his or her life. It defined 'euthanasia' as 'a deliberate intervention undertaken with the express intention of ending a life to relieve intractable suffering' (a definition which should be extended to include any reason that death is thought to benefit the patient). My focus is, therefore, *actions* rather than omissions which shorten life. This focus does not (as will become clear) deny the possibility of intentional killing or assisting suicide by omission, but simply reflects the current debate. Campaigners for decriminalisation are pressing for doctors to be allowed to administer lethal injections, currently prohibited by the law of murder, and/or to prescribe lethal prescriptions, currently prohibited by the law against assisting suicide. Other Committee definitions I shall adopt concern the presence or absence of a request by the patient. 'Euthanasia' is:

– 'voluntary' when carried out at the patient's request (which I shall refer to as 'VAE': voluntary, active euthanasia);
– 'non-voluntary' when the patient does not have the capacity to make a request ('NVAE': non-voluntary, active euthanasia), and
– 'involuntary' when the patient is competent to make a request but does not do so ('IVAE': involuntary, active euthanasia).[2]

III. TEN ARGUMENTS FOR DECRIMINALISATION

Let us now consider 10 arguments which have been advanced in favour of decriminalising VAE/PAS. Each argument will be briefly stated and then followed by counter-arguments. First, respect for autonomy.

A. Autonomy

The decriminalisation of VAE/PAS is required out of respect for individual autonomy. Patients have a right to make their own decisions about the time and manner of their death. Whose life is it anyway?

i. Autonomy vs the Inviolability of Life

The principle of 'respect for autonomy' has in recent years become for many a core if not dominant principle of biomedical ethics. It is not, however, unproblematic. Its advocates often fail

---

[2] *Report of the Select Committee on Medical Ethics* (HL 1993–94, 21-I) (hereafter 'Walton') paras 20–26.

to agree on precisely what constitutes an 'autonomous' choice or to offer any convincing account of why respect for someone else's choice as such should be regarded as a moral principle, let alone a core or dominant moral principle. Our capacity for choice is undoubtedly important, for it is through our choices that we shape our lives and influence the lives of those around us, for good or for ill. But we should exercise that capacity responsibly by choosing for good, not ill. The advice 'Be careful what you wish for because you might get it' is not bereft of wisdom: consider King Midas. As Professor Gormally and I have put it:

> Autonomy itself as a capacity is to be valued *precisely in so far as its exercise makes for the well-being and flourishing of the human beings who possess it*. But it is plain that many exercises of the capacity, that is, many self-determining choices, are destructive of human well-being – both in the life of the chooser and in the lives of others affected by his or her choices. The mere fact that someone has *chosen* to act or to be treated in a certain way establishes no title to moral respect for what has been chosen. The character of the choice must satisfy certain criteria in order to warrant our respect. The most basic criterion is that a choice should be consistent with respect for the fundamental dignity both of the chooser and of others.[3]

Neither Anglo-American law nor professional medical ethics have ever held that the mere fact *that* I have chosen justifies *what* I have chosen. English law refuses to respect various choices, however autonomous. It disallows choices to be owned, eaten or executed, to buy illicit drugs or to drive while not wearing a seatbelt. In the medical context patients have no right to demand whatever treatments or drugs they may want. A doctor may not amputate a healthy limb, even on request. Female genital mutilation (FGM) is prohibited by the Female Genital Mutilation Act 2003, regardless of the woman's consent. The Mental Health Act 1983 allows treatment for mental disorder to be imposed on a competent

---

[3] J Keown and L Gormally, 'Human Dignity, Autonomy and Mentally Incapacitated Patients: A Critique of *Who Decides?*' (1999) 4 *Web Journal of Current Legal Issues*, part II. See also RP George, *Making Men Moral* (Oxford, Oxford University Press, 1993).

patient who chooses against it. None of these autonomous choices need involve a risk of harm to anyone except the person making them, but they are nevertheless disallowed by the law. Other autonomous choices do involve a risk of harm to others, which helps explain why they too are rejected by the law even when, as with duelling, the risk of harm may be entirely consensual. Simply to claim, therefore, that patients have a 'right to choose' VAE/PAS because it is 'their life' begs the moral question. The focus of our moral enquiry should not be some question-begging 'right to choose' but on what it is *right* to choose, on which choices merit, or do not merit, respect. Choices which undermine human flourishing, such as choices to kill or mutilate (whether oneself or another) simply lack moral justification. Further, given that our capacity for autonomy *is* so valuable, how can it be right deliberately to extinguish it by deliberately extinguishing its bearer? Must liberty not at least sometimes be limited in order to be possessed?

One limit is the cardinal ethical principle of the inviolability of life. (It is often referred to as the 'sanctity' of life, but 'sanctity' has distracting religious overtones: as we shall see, the principle can stand on solely philosophical grounds.) This historic principle, foundational to Western criminal law and professional medical ethics, holds that it is wrong intentionally to kill other people (at least if they are, like patients, not involved in unjust aggression). The principle is grounded in the recognition of the inherent dignity of each human being. The Preamble to the Universal Declaration of Human Rights (1948) proclaims that 'recognition of the inherent dignity and of the equal and inalienable rights of all members of the human family is the foundation of freedom, justice and peace in the world'. The Preamble has it right. Each of us shares an 'inherent dignity' and enjoys 'equal and inalienable rights' in virtue of our common membership of the human family. Human life is, like friendship and knowledge, a self-evident good and is, like them, a basic rather than an instrumental good. It is a basic element of human well-being, not merely a vehicle for a life of sufficient 'quality' or 'worth'. We *all* share a fundamental equality-in-dignity, regardless of our abilities or disabilities. There is no one whose life is 'not worth living', no one who would be 'better off dead', there are no 'second class' patients. The lives of *all* patients are worthwhile, even if some patients lose sight of their worth.

To say that human life is a basic good is *not*, however, to say that it is the highest good and should be preserved at all costs. That would be 'vitalism' and morally indefensible. We all enjoy a 'right to life' but that is primarily *a right not to be intentionally killed*. Applying the well-established ethical principle of 'double effect' (of which more later), it is proper for a doctor to administer palliative drugs to ease the pain of the dying, even if the doctor foresees that the drugs will as a side-effect shorten life. It is also permissible to withhold or withdraw treatments which are 'futile' (that is, offer no reasonable hope of therapeutic benefit) or which are too burdensome to the patient, even if the doctor foresees that without them the patient will die sooner. If, therefore, a treatment cannot improve a patient's medical condition or 'quality of life', it need not be given, even though it might prolong life. There is nothing necessarily wrong with merely foreseeing the shortening of life, and even with welcoming the natural end to suffering which death may bring. Here an important caveat must be mentioned concerning the term 'quality of life'. The concept can be used, as we have just used it, to refer to the patient's medical condition as a baseline for deciding whether a particular treatment is likely to improve that condition. This usage is consistent with inviolability, for it is concerned with judging whether a *treatment* would be worthwhile. But the words 'quality of life' are sometimes used in a way that is inconsistent with inviolability, as a way of judging whether the patient's *life* is worthwhile. Take a frail, elderly cancer patient who is only hours from death. It is one thing to say that, given the patient's 'quality of life' (close to death from terminal cancer) life-prolonging *treatment* (such as cardiopulmonary resuscitation) would be futile. It is quite another to say that, given the patient's 'quality of life', the patient's *life* is futile, that the patient would be 'better off dead'. To use 'quality of life' in the latter sense is to invite euthanasia.

The principle of the inviolability of life has long been instantiated in English law. Accordingly, the law does not require doctors to do everything possible to extend patients' lives. It recognises that patients have the right to refuse treatments which offer no reasonable hope of benefit or which they would find too burdensome, and that doctors may administer palliative drugs even if they shorten life as an unintended side-effect. But while patient autonomy gives us a right to refuse procedures, it does not give us a right to demand them; it is a shield, not a sword. In particular, the law rightly holds that we have no right to be killed, or to be helped to kill ourselves, whether or not we are dying and whether or not we want to die. Patient autonomy yields to the inviolability of life. Were it otherwise, VAE/PAS would long ago have been lawful. The inviolability of life has also informed instruments on human rights. Article 2(1) of the European Convention on Human Rights (1950) provides: 'Everyone's right to life shall be protected by law. No one shall be deprived of his life intentionally . . .'. In 1999 the Parliamentary Assembly of the Council of Europe passed Recommendation 1418 on the 'Protection of the human rights and dignity of the terminally ill and the dying' which called on the Council of Europe to respect and protect the dignity of the terminally ill by upholding the prohibition on intentionally taking their lives, even on request.[4] The inviolability principle was cited by the Walton Committee as a major reason for its rejection of VAE/PAS. Having evaluated the arguments for decriminalisation, the Committee concluded:

> [W]e do not believe that these arguments are sufficient reason to weaken society's prohibition on intentional killing. That prohibition is the cornerstone of law and of social relationships. It protects each one of us impartially, embodying the belief that all are equal.[5]

---

[4] http://assembly.coe.int/main.asp?link=/Documents/AdoptedText/ta99/EREC1418.htm.

[5] Walton (n 2) para 237.

ii. The Autonomous Few vs The Vulnerable Many

A second counter-argument is that decriminalisation would prejudice the vulnerable, both those who are autonomous and those who are not. Some vulnerable patients, such as the frail elderly, might be pressured into requesting VAE/PAS. Or they might simply be made to feel a burden by their relatives and by society. How we feel about ourselves can, of course, be hugely influenced by how others feel toward us. And the dying, the disabled and the disadvantaged are hardly cherished by modern society.

Concerns about the vulnerable have figured prominently among expert bodies which have considered the case for decriminalisation. The Walton Committee concluded:

> [W]e do not think it possible to set secure limits on voluntary euthanasia . . . It would be next to impossible to ensure that all acts of euthanasia were truly voluntary, and that any liberalisation of the law was not abused . . . These dangers are such that we believe that any decriminalisation of voluntary euthanasia would give rise to more, and more grave, problems than those it sought to address.[6]

It continued:

> We are also concerned that vulnerable people – the elderly, lonely, sick or distressed – would feel pressure, whether real or imagined, to request early death . . . [T]he message which society sends to vulnerable and disadvantaged people should not, however obliquely, encourage them to seek death, but should assure them of our care and support in life.[7]

A contemporaneous report was produced by the New York State Task Force on Life and the Law. Some of the Task Force's members supported VAE/PAS in principle, but even they joined its unanimous conclusion that decriminalisation would be 'unwise and dangerous public policy'. Its report declared:

> After lengthy deliberations, the Task Force unanimously concluded that the dangers of such a dramatic change in public policy would far

[6] ibid, para 238.
[7] ibid, para 239.

outweigh any possible benefits. In light of the pervasive failure of our health care system to treat pain and diagnose and treat depression, legalizing assisted suicide and euthanasia would be profoundly dangerous for many individuals who are ill and vulnerable. The risks would be most severe for those who are elderly, poor, socially disadvantaged, or without access to good medical care.[8]

The Task Force's concerns have been echoed by the philosopher Onora O'Neill. As Baroness O'Neill she was a prominent opponent in the House of Lords of Lord Joffe's Assisted Dying for the Terminally Ill Bill, which sought to decriminalise PAS. She observed:

> Legalising 'assisted dying' places a huge burden on the vulnerable, let alone on the vulnerable and depressed. Although we can all imagine cases of highly confident persons who are immune from these feelings, we are all familiar with the commonplace realities of dependence and vulnerability. We should not worsen the situation of the vulnerable by making it easy to point them to the door. Laws are written for all of us in all situations – not just for the unusually independent.

She concluded:

> Legalising 'assisted dying' amounts to adopting a principle of indifference towards a special and acute form of vulnerability: in order to allow a few independent folk to get others to kill them on demand, we are to be indifferent to the fact that many less independent people would come under pressure to request the same. Indifference to others may appeal to those with an exalted view of their own independence, but it is not a principle for those who are vulnerable and need others' help.[9]

These concerns should not be lightly dismissed, particularly as discrimination against the elderly and disabled, even in wealthy nations such as the UK and US, is a harsh reality. Age discrimination in the

---

[8] New York State Task Force on Life and the Law, *When Death is Sought: Assisted Suicide and Euthanasia in the Medical Context* (New York, NYSTF, 1994) ix.

[9] Baroness O'Neill of Bengarve, 'A Note on Autonomy and Assisted Dying' (memorandum circulated to members of the House of Lords during their consideration of the Joffe Bill).

provision of healthcare is well-documented and extends beyond the denial of treatment to the denial of even basic care. The scandal at the Mid-Staffordshire Hospital in recent years has exposed shocking abuse and neglect in the NHS. The chairman of the official inquiry observed that many patients suffered 'horrific experiences that will haunt them and their loved ones for the rest of their lives'. He explained:

> for many patients the most basic elements of care were neglected. Calls for help to use the bathroom were ignored and patients were left lying in soiled sheeting and sitting on commodes for hours, often feeling ashamed and afraid. Patients were left unwashed, at times for up to a month. Food and drinks were left out of the reach of patients and many were forced to rely on family members for help with feeding. Staff failed to make basic observations and pain relief was provided late or in some cases not at all.[10]

A recent survey of NHS hospitals by the Care Quality Commission found that one quarter failed to provide basic care to the elderly. Some patients were even prescribed water by their doctors because they had been left to go thirsty by their nurses.[11] In the US, the National Elder Abuse Incidence Study published in 1998 concluded that over half a million elderly people in domestic settings had been victims of abuse, neglect or self-neglect in 1996, and that almost 80 per cent of cases went unreported. The bulk of abuse and neglect was by relatives.

The disabled are also victims of discrimination. Baroness Jane Campbell wrote that if Lord Joffe's Bill were enacted, 'None of us will be safe'.[12] She pointed out that not a single disability rights organisation supported the Bill. In 2009 she opposed an amendment proposed by Lord Falconer to the Coroners and Justice Bill, an amendment which would have decriminalised helping the ter-

---

[10] 'Final Report Of The Independent Inquiry Into Care Provided By Mid Staffordshire NHS Foundation Trust', www.midstaffsinquiry.com/pressrelease.html.

[11] M Beckford, 'Hospitals Failing to Provide Basic Care for Elderly' *The Daily Telegraph* (26 May 2011).

[12] J Campbell, 'Stop Trying to Kill us Off' *The Guardian* (9 May 2006).

minally ill to travel to a jurisdiction where so-called 'assisted dying' is lawful. She wrote that PAS fed into the stereotype that the disabled led such burdensome lives that they must want to die, when the reality was: 'We want help to live – not help to die'. She added:

> Those of us who know what it is to be disabled with a terminal condition are fearful that the tide has already turned against us. If I should ever seek death at those times when my progressive condition challenges me, I want to know that you are there supporting my continued life and its value. The last thing I want is for you to give up on me, especially when I need you the most.[13]

She was the lead signatory of a letter from a battery of disability rights groups, from both the UK and the US, opposing the Falconer proposal. The letter read:

> A law decriminalizing assisted suicide would undoubtedly place disabled people under pressure to end their lives early to relieve the burden on relatives, carers or the state.

It continued:

> The concerns are not side issues that only affect disabled people. We are like society's 'canaries in the coalmine' who can often see the dangers of potentially discriminatory legislation before others, as it impacts on us even before the deed is done. We are scared now; we will be terrified if assisted suicide becomes state-sanctioned.[14]

Their concerns are unlikely to be assuaged by comments from some leading 'right to die' advocates. Baroness Mary Warnock, perhaps the most influential ethicist in British government circles, has stated: 'If you're demented, you're wasting people's lives – your family's lives – and you're wasting the resources of the National Health Service'. She suggested that there was nothing wrong with people feeling they ought to die because they felt a burden on the state. She added that it was to be hoped that, if one became incapacitated, one's proxy would be able to ask for one's

---

[13] J Campbell, 'Assisted Dying: Not in our Name' *The Guardian* (7 July 2009).
[14] Baroness Campbell et al, 'Open Letter from Leaders of Disabled People's Movement in UK and USA', www.carenotkilling.org.uk/?show=775 .

death to be hastened because one would not wish to live in that condition. She forecast:

> I think that's the way the future will go, putting it rather brutally, you'd be licensing people to put others down. Actually I think why not, because the real person has gone already and all that's left is just the body of a person, and nobody wants to be remembered in this condition.[15]

Her comments outraged disability groups, but her prediction would likely prove all too accurate were we to decriminalise VAE/PAS. A book edited by leading US 'right to die' advocate Professor Margaret Battin contains an honest prediction by one expert that if PAS (to which the expert expresses no opposition) is decriminalised,

> strong social expectations are likely to develop for individuals to choose assisted suicide as soon as their physical capacities decline to a point where they become extremely dependent upon others in an expensive, inconvenient way.[16]

The 'right to die' would surely in time become more of a 'duty to die', not least given the burgeoning costs of caring for a growing elderly and demented population. It is often said that the true test of a society is how well it treats its most vulnerable members. The very fact of decriminalisation could easily by itself signal to vulnerable groups, directly or indirectly, not only that they *may* seek an earlier death, but that they *should*. A witness appearing before a Canadian Senate Committee (which went on to reject decriminalisation) put this point well:

> Canada has identified a suicide problem among its youth, and we have responded 'How can we prevent it?' Canada has identified a suicide problem among Aboriginal peoples and we have responded 'How can we prevent it?' Canada has identified a suicide problem among people with disabilities and we have responded 'How can we assist them to kill themselves?'[17]

---

[15] Jackie Macadam, 'A Duty to Die?' *Life and Work* (October 2008) 23, 24–25.

[16] PS Mann, 'Meanings of Death' in M Battin et al (eds), *Physician-Assisted Suicide: Expanding the Debate* (New York, Routledge, 1998) 11, 25.

[17] J Keown, *Euthanasia, Ethics and Public Policy* (Cambridge, Cambridge University Press, 2002) 280.

The Select Committee which considered the Joffe Bill, which was chaired by former Lord Chancellor Lord Mackay and which reported in 2005, endorsed Baroness O'Neill's view that those who would want PAS are a few, independently minded people. The report noted:

> There was general agreement among our witnesses that the number of people who might be regarded as serious about ending their lives, who are not psychiatrically ill and who are unlikely to be deflected from their purpose is *very small indeed* and comprises to a large extent terminally ill people who have strong personalities and a history of being in control of their lives and whose suffering derives more from the fact of their terminal illness and from the loss of control which this involves than from the symptoms of their disease.[18]

Would it be right to jeopardise the many vulnerable members of our society including the dying, the demented, the disabled and the disadvantaged, whose numbers are set to grow as our population inexorably ages, to accommodate the desire of a tiny minority to control the timing of their death? Why do the wishes of a few to control the time of their death trump the interests of the many in not being killed, particularly by malice or mistake?

iii. How Autonomous?

How autonomous would requests for VAE/PAS be? Even requests which were not compromised by pressure from grasping or uncaring or exhausted relatives might not be truly autonomous: there is an established link between requests for VAE/PAS and clinical depression. In a key statement against the Joffe Bill the Royal College of Psychiatrists observed that studies of the terminally ill had clearly shown that depression is strongly associated with the desire for a hastened death, including VAE/PAS, and that once a patients' depression is effectively treated, 98–99 per cent change their mind about wanting die. It also cautioned:

---

[18] *Report of the Select Committee on the Assisted Dying for the Terminally Ill Bill* (HL 2004–05, 86-I) (hereafter 'Mackay') para 244. Emphasis added.

Many doctors do not recognise depression or know how to assess for its presence in terminally ill patients . . . Even when recognized, doctors often take the view that 'understandable depression' cannot be treated, does not count or is in some way not real depression.[19]

The Royal College was 'deeply worried' by the Bill and concluded that requests for PAS should trigger effective treatment of depression and its causes, not PAS.

The vulnerability of the suicidal was recently illustrated by the conviction in the United States of William Melchert-Dinkel, who advised depressed people over the internet how to commit suicide. His victims included a 32-year-old Briton who hanged himself and an 18-year-old Canadian who threw herself into an icy river and drowned.

iv. Some Patients 'Better Off Dead'?

Decriminalising VAE/PAS would not only allow doctors to act on requests which were in practice compromised by pressure or depression. It would also lead in logic to the decriminalisation of NVAE. This is because, despite the emphasis campaigners place on autonomy, the case for VAE/PAS rests at least as much on the belief that some patients are (because of terminal illness, suffering or whatever) 'better off dead'. Campaigners are not proposing that VAE/PAS should be available simply because the patient has made an autonomous request. According to their own standard proposals, doctors would have to decide whether the patient's autonomous request should be granted. And how would the doctor decide *other than on the basis of a belief that death would benefit the patient?* In the Netherlands, which has permitted VAE/PAS for over a quarter of a century, doctors refuse more requests from patients than they endorse. This illustrates the decisive role played by the *doctor's* decision that death would, or would not, benefit the patient. A doctor who is prepared to make such a judgement

---

[19] Statement from the Royal College of Psychiatrists on Physician-Assisted Suicide (2006) para 2.4, www.rcpsych.ac.uk/pressparliament/collegeresponses/ physicianassistedsuicide.aspx. The guidance is currently under review.

forfeits any principled objection to NVAE. *For: if death would bene-fit the patient, why deprive the patient of that benefit merely because the patient cannot request it?* Is a doctor not duty-bound to benefit his or her patient, competent or incompetent?

While most philosophers who advocate VAE also openly endorse NVAE, a few have tried to refute the logical link between the two. Hallvard Lillehammer has argued:

> The defender of voluntary euthanasia should claim that moral weight attaches *both* to the patient's autonomous request . . . *and* to the doc-tor's competent judgment that death would be a benefit to the patient.[20]

On this view, he adds, both are '*individually necessary*, and *jointly suf-ficient*, conditions for permissible voluntary euthanasia'.[21] This is more assertion than argument. *Why* are both necessary? Even if autonomy is a reason *for* VAE, its absence is not a reason *against* NVAE. If a patient requests a lethal injection to put an end to suffering, the doctor may cite autonomy and beneficence as two reasons for providing it. If the suffering patient is incompetent, the doctor still has one reason – beneficence – to provide it.

Professor John Griffiths, a leading expert on and defender of Dutch euthanasia, has also attempted to refute the logical slope. He rightly notes that in VAE a second person, the doctor, is involved and that the doctor requires more to justify VAE than the patient's request. The justification, he adds, lies in the doctor's duty to relieve suffering. Why, then, may this same duty not justify NVAE? Griffiths answers: 'The requirement of a request will not be swept away precisely because it is based on an entirely different principle'.[22] The principle of respect for autonomy is indeed a dif-ferent principle, but it is simply *irrelevant* in the case of an incom-petent patient (at least if that patient has never expressed a wish about what they would have wanted). As we shall see, just as

---

[20] H Lillehammer, 'Voluntary Euthanasia and the Logical Slippery Slope Argument' [2002] 61(3) *Cambridge Law Journal* 545, 548.

[21] ibid.

[22] J Griffiths et al, *Euthanasia and Law in Europe* (Oxford, Hart, 2008) 514.

Dutch courts invoked the doctor's duty to alleviate suffering to justify VAE, they have more recently invoked the very same duty to justify NVAE. Discussing the Dutch courts' endorsement of infanticide, Griffiths writes:

> The applicable norms in the Netherlands have assuredly changed in the direction of open acceptance of the legitimacy of termination of life of severely defective newborn babies . . . [T]he influence on these changes of the way euthanasia had earlier been legalised and regulated is obvious. In this sense, one might speak of a normative slippery slope.[23]

The justification invoked by the Dutch courts for their endorsement of NVAE – that the doctor's duty to relieve suffering applies even if the patient is incompetent – precisely tracks the logical argument that even if autonomy is not in play, beneficence is. The courts' reasoning, far from being a refutation of the logical argument, is a vivid illustration of it. Griffiths' rejection of the logical slope is, therefore, puzzling. It is, indeed, doubly puzzling, for he appears, like many supporters of VAE, to have no objection to NVAE. He even suggests that both should be classified as 'normal medical practice' and that doctors should only have to report them to other doctors, confidentially. In view of the force of the logical argument it is not surprising that some other leading defenders of VAE in the Netherlands have broken ranks and openly endorsed it. Professor Paul van der Maas and colleagues, authors of important national surveys into end of life practice in the Netherlands (which we shall mention later), have written:

> [I]s it not true that once one accepts [voluntary] euthanasia and assisted suicide, the principle of universalizability forces one to accept termination of life without explicit request, at least in some circumstances, as well? In our view the answer to this question must be affirmative.[24]

As the logical slippery slope argument shows, permitting VAE/ PAS is no 'private' matter concerning only a few highly autono-

---

[23]   ibid 252.
[24]   Keown (n 17) 123.

mous patients. It clearly has profound ramifications for the well-being of *all* patients who might be judged 'better off dead', not least those who are unable to refuse it.

v. *Autonomy's 'Slippery Slope'*

The previous counter-argument is often resisted by VAE/PAS campaigners on the ground that it is not the doctor who decides whether the patient's life is no longer worth living, but the patient. As we have just seen, however, this retort fails. Under the proposals they themselves put forward, the patient's autonomous request is by itself insufficient. But even if the retort were sound it would lead to another, no less precipitous, slope. *For: if the patient's own assessment were decisive, why would it not justify VAE/PAS for anyone who believed that they would be better off dead, whether terminally ill or not and whether suffering unbearably or not?*

B. Compassion

Doctors and nurses should treat patients with compassion. VAE/PAS should, therefore, be made available to terminally ill patients as a way of putting an end to suffering which they no longer want to endure. We put suffering animals out of their misery, why not suffering patients?

i. *Is Compassion a Moral Principle?*

Compassion is a laudable emotion, but it is not a moral principle. We should feel compassion for the poor, but that would hardly justify robbing banks to redistribute wealth. And advocates of VAE/PAS have no monopoly on compassion. Some of the most compassionate members of the medical and nursing professions are to be found among those who care for the terminally ill, and they are among the strongest opponents of VAE/PAS. They have long realised that their duty to alleviate their patients' suffering is not a duty to end their suffering at any price. They recognise that true com-passion, true 'suffering with' the patient, means caring, not killing; affirming, not denying, the patient's worth; promoting solidarity, not suicide. Moreover, if we were to allow VAE/PAS out of 'compassion' for the terminally ill, how often would our compassion turn out on closer analysis to be counterfeit: a desire not to put them out of *their* misery, but to put them out of *our* misery? What of the argument that because we put down suffering animals we should therefore end the lives of patients? The argument is surely valid, but only if we want to treat patients like animals. It may be also argued that although compassion is not a moral principle, beneficence – the duty to benefit others – is. But while it is obvious that palliative care to ease suffering benefits patients, it is far from obvious that killing patients, depriving them of their very existence, benefits them. A patient's *suffering* is bad, but that does not mean that their *life* is bad.

ii. Compassion's 'Slippery Slope'

If compassion justified us in giving a lethal prescription to a terminally ill patient on request to end their suffering, it would equally justify us in giving them a lethal injection, particularly if they were physically unable to commit suicide. It would also justify us in giving a lethal injection to a terminally ill patient who was incapable of making a request. And what about patients who are suffering but not terminally ill, such those with chronic arthritis? Why should *they* be denied the 'compassion' of a hastened death, when they have longer to suffer than those who are dying?

iii. Palliative Care

VAE/PAS is by no means the only way to respond to the suffering of the terminally ill: there is the real alternative of palliative care. In the UK, where the late Dame Cicely Saunders founded the hospice movement in 1967, palliative care is a recognised specialism, unlike in other countries such as the US and the Netherlands. In 2008 the Department of Health launched a National End of Life Care Strategy for England to promote high-quality care for all adults approaching the end of life. In 2010 a report by *The Economist* ranked the UK first in the provision of quality care for the dying. Much still needs to be done to ensure that high-quality end-of-life care is available to all, but it is clear that never before have doctors and nurses been able to do so much to relieve the suffering of so many. We should therefore ask not only whether VAE/PAS is ethical, but whether it can even claim to be needed. In England in 2006 over 70 per cent of members of the Royal College of Physicians (and 95 per cent of those in the specialism of palliative medicine) agreed with the following statement:

> *[W]ith improvements in palliative care, good clinical care can be provided within existing legislation and . . . patients can die with dignity. A change in legislation is not needed.*[25]

In the view of the medical profession, then, VAE/PAS is simply 'not needed' to enable patients to die with dignity.

There is also a real risk that decriminalising VAE/PAS would distract from the urgent task of making palliative and social care available to all who need them. Why fund palliative and social care, policymakers would surely ask, if there were a quicker, cheaper alternative? In debate on the Joffe Bill, a former health minister commented that 'it is an inescapable fact that ultimately policy is driven by money', adding that the 'stark fact is that palliative care is expensive and a lethal pill is cheap'.[26] In 2009 Dr Borst, who steered legislation regulating VAE/PAS through the Dutch parliament in 2001, told researcher Dr Anne-Marie The that a decline in the quality of care for the terminally ill had followed. Dr The has stated that palliative care is so poor that patients 'often ask for euthanasia out of fear' of dying in agony.[27] If that can happen in a developed country like the Netherlands,

[25] 'RCP cannot support legal change on assisted dying – survey results', www.rcplondon.ac.uk/news/news.asp?PR_id=310.

[26] HL Deb, vol 681, cols 1213–14 (Lord Elton).

[27] S Caldwell, 'Now Dutch Turn Against Legalised Mercy Killing' *The Daily Mail* (9 December 2009).

which boasts comprehensive healthcare coverage, why could it not happen in countries like the UK and the US?

iv. The Healing Vocation of Doctors

The medical profession regards helping patients to commit suicide as contrary to its vocation to heal. Healing means to restore to health, to make whole or sound. The first purpose of medicine is to restore patients to health, or at least to some approximation of health and, if that is not possible, to treat symptoms such as pain. But to kill means to destroy; it is the antithesis of making healthy or whole. This is why doctors who abuse their power over life and death, like Dr Mengele or Dr Shipman, attract especial opprobrium: they have betrayed their healing vocation. It is also a major reason why VAE/PAS has long been rejected by the British Medical Association, the American Medical Association and the World Medical Association

The medical profession has also expressed the reasonable fear that decriminalisation would lead to an erosion of trust between doctor and patient. In its evidence to the Mackay Committee, the General Medical Council cautioned that a change in the law to allow PAS would have profound implications for the role and responsibilities of doctors and their relationships with their patients. Similarly, Professor Steve Field, Chair of the Royal College of General Practitioners, has written:

> If we doctors take on the additional role of taking life . . . it would undermine our credibility, undermine the trust between the patient and doctor and adversely affect the doctor-patient relationship.[28]

As Professor Alexander Capron, the leading US health lawyer, vividly put it, he would not like to have to guess whether the doctor who approached his bedside was wearing the white coat of the healer or the black hood of the executioner.

---

[28] S Field, 'Why assisted suicide has no place in the UK' *The Guardian* (22 June 2009).

Euthanasia advocates often claim that the level of trust in doctors is high in the Netherlands: we shall respond to this point when we consider the Dutch experience. They could also invoke the Royal College of Nursing's recent shift to a 'neutral' stance on PAS. However, as Baroness Emerton, a former Chief Nursing Officer, has pointed out, the shift followed a consultation process which reflected the views of only 0.3 per cent of its membership. She observed: 'it looks very much as though the RCN Council is using a microscopic sample of nursing opinion to steer the college on to a politically controversial course'.[29]

C. Legal Hypocrisy

When a doctor administers drugs to palliate pain, foreseeing they will shorten life, this is morally the same as administering drugs with intent to kill. Yet the law, hypocritically, permits the former and prohibits the latter. The law is equally hypocritical in allowing (indeed requiring) a doctor to withdraw life support at a patient's request but not to provide the patient with a prescription for lethal drugs or to give the patient a lethal injection.

i. Intention vs Foresight

Intention is, in ordinary English, different from foresight. You may buy a lottery ticket intending to win without foreseeing that you will. Conversely, you may foresee the discomfort of having a tooth extracted without intending it. The distinction is not only linguistic but moral. It is always wrong intentionally to bring about a bad consequence; it is not always wrong foreseeably to do so. If we make a bad consequence our aim, we endorse it, and that endorsement corrupts our character. Though we can always avoid intending bad consequences, we cannot always avoid foreseeably bringing them about, either by our actions or our omissions. Bad side-effects are often an inevitable part of our good

---

[29] Baroness Emerton, 'A dangerous road for nurses to tread' *The Times* (29 July 2009).

purposes. The euthanasiast doctor who intentionally hastens a patient's death judges that the patient's life is no longer worth living, and turns from healer to killer. The doctor who aims to alleviate pain, merely foreseeing that life will be shortened as a side-effect, does neither. Though we are morally responsible for all the effects of our actions, good and bad, intended or foreseen, we may not be blameworthy for the foreseen bad effects of our conduct. The morality of our actions is not, then, simply about the effects we bring about: it is also about our state of mind, not least our intention. Though the impact may be identical, there is a moral difference between accidentally tripping over someone and deliberately kicking him. Even a dog, it has been aptly said, knows the difference between being tripped over and being kicked. The moral importance of our state of mind is reflected in the criminal law. Criminal conviction for serious offences generally requires not simply that we have brought about a bad consequence but that we have done so intentionally (by aiming to bring it about) or recklessly (by consciously taking an unjustified risk of bringing it about).

The principle of 'double effect' tells us when our conduct is morally justified even though it will bring about bad as well as good effects. The principle holds that it is permissible to bring about a foreseen bad consequence if the bad effect is not intended as an end or a means, and the foreseeable causing of the side-effect does not violate other moral norms, especially fairness. It is often expressed in terms of four conditions:

– our conduct must not be wrong in itself;
– we must intend only the good effect, not the bad effect;
– the bad effect must not be the means to the good effect;
– there must be a proportionate reason for allowing the bad effect to occur.

'Double effect' therefore condones the administration of palliative drugs if the doctor's intention is to alleviate a dying patient's pain, even if the doctor foresees that as a side-effect the drugs will hasten the patient's death. First, palliating pain is not wrong in itself. Secondly, the doctor intends to ease pain, not to shorten life. Thirdly, the shortening of life is not a means to the easing of pain. Fourthly, easing the pain of a patient who is near death anyway is a sufficient reason for allowing the hastening of death. It would obviously be different if the doctor sought to ease the pain *by* shortening life. That would be wrong in itself, the doctor would intend the bad effect, and the bad effect would be a means to the good effect. It would also be different if the doctor administered life-shortening drugs to a healthy patient for a hangover: easing a hangover is hardly a sufficient reason for foreseeably shortening life. Critics of 'double effect' sometimes misrepresent the fourth condition as 'consequentialist', that is, as adopting a moral approach which holds that morality is solely about maximising good consequences, that the end justifies the means. However, as its first three conditions make plain, 'double effect' only makes sense as part of an ethical approach which regards certain conduct as always wrong, regardless of the consequences. To take the consequences of one's action into account does not make one a 'consequentialist'. It is simply prudent, and there is no conflict between being principled and being prudent. Adherents of the inviolability of life can oppose the decriminalisation of VAE/PAS not only because it would be wrong in principle, but also because it would have adverse consequences in practice.

'Double effect' has long been established in professional medical ethics and in the law. In the *Bland* case, Lord Goff referred to:

> the established rule that a doctor may, when caring for a patient who is, for example, dying of cancer, lawfully administer painkilling drugs despite the fact that he knows that an incidental effect of that application will be to abbreviate the patient's life.[30]

As his Lordship had explained on a previous occasion:

> [T]here can be foresight of consequences without intention. To take an example . . .: when Field Marshal Montgomery invaded France on D-Day, he foresaw that many of the troops under his command

---

[30] *Airedale NHS Trust v Bland* [1993] AC 789, 867.

would be killed on that very day. Obviously, however, he did not intend that any of them should be killed.[31]

When in 1997 the then Attorney-General, Lord Williams of Mostyn, was asked whether the government was satisfied with the current state of the criminal law and medical practice in relation to the palliative treatment of terminally ill patients, he replied that the government *was* satisfied. Citing Lord Goff's statement in the *Bland* case, Lord Williams commented that he did not think doctors had the slightest difficulty understanding the distinction between intending death and merely foreseeing death. He added that the law was neither difficult nor obscure; it was 'perfectly plain'.[32] Although it is true to say that the English courts have sometimes come close to equating intention with foresight of virtual certainty they have, as Professor Peter Skegg has pointed out, 'tended to say that foresight of virtual certainty is something from which intention may be found or inferred, and . . . have stopped short of saying that such foresight is itself a form of intent'.[33]

US law also recognises the moral difference between intending and merely foreseeing death. The Supreme Court, in its two landmark decisions in 1997 rejecting a constitutional challenge to laws against assisting suicide, distinguished between withdrawing life-prolonging treatment on request, which need involve no intention to facilitate death, and writing a prescription for lethal drugs.[34] Even the Dutch, the pioneers of VAE/PAS, accept that intention is the badge of euthanasia. For example, their national surveys of medical practice at the end of life have consistently defined euthanasia in terms of intending, not foreseeing, the hastening of death.

---

[31] R Goff, 'The Mental Element in the Crime of Murder' (1988) 104 *Law Quarterly Review* 30, 44.

[32] HL Deb, vol 583, cols 742–44.

[33] PDG Skegg, 'Medical Acts Hastening Death' in PDG Skegg et al (eds), *Medical Law in New Zealand* (Wellington, Thomson Brookers, 2006) 505, 524.

[34] *Washington v Glucksberg* 521 US 702 at 725–26; *Vacco, Attorney-General of New York et al v Quill et al* 521 US 793 at 800–03.

It is true that in the *Bland* case the Law Lords held it lawful to withdraw tube-feeding from a patient in a persistent vegetative state (PVS), even though a majority of their Lordships thought that the doctor's intention was to kill the patient. However, a doctor's intention in withdrawing tube-feeding need not be to shorten life, and may only be to stop what the doctor regards (whether rightly or wrongly is another matter) as a 'futile medical treatment' which could not restore the patient to health or well-functioning. Indeed Lord Goff drew an analogy between withdrawing tube-feeding from a patient in PVS and switching off a ventilator. Moreover, if the case does hold that in such cases doctors may intentionally kill by omission, it is bad law. Lord Mustill commented that it left the law in a 'morally and intellectually mis-shapen' state, prohibiting intentional killing by the administration of a lethal injection but permitting it by the withdrawal of tube-feeding. The majority thereby dug themselves into a hole. But this is not a reason to keep digging and to permit active intentional killing. It a reason to stop digging, get out of the hole and fill it in. Fortunately, the hole may well have been filled by Parliament. Section 4(5) of the Mental Capacity Act 2005 provides that in considering whether life-sustaining treatment is in the 'best interests' of an incompetent patient, the person making the determination must not be 'motivated by a desire to bring about his death'. (A similar phrase in the Insolvency Act 1986 has been interpreted by the courts to mean intent or purpose.[35])

Some reject the distinction between intention and foresight because of the forensic challenge of ascertaining what a doctor intended. This objection was given short shrift by the Walton Committee, which noted that juries are asked every day to assess intention in all sorts of cases.

In short, Anglo-American law and professional medical ethics have long drawn an important distinction, recognised by sound philosophy and common sense, between the intended and the

---

[35] See J Finnis, 'The Mental Capacity Act 2005: Some Ethical and Legal Issues' in H Watt (ed), *Incapacity and Care* (Oxford, The Linacre Centre, 2009) 95 at 101–02.

merely foreseen hastening of death. To conflate euthanasia with palliative treatment is to elide a crucial distinction. The conflation not only causes confusion but would have dire consequences if adopted by the law: it would render doctors who practise good palliative medicine which incidentally shortens life liable for murder.

ii. Causation

The accusation of legal hypocrisy may also be questioned on the ground that the administration of palliative drugs or the withdrawal of treatment in accordance with good medical practice are not a *cause* of death. Like the distinction between intention and foresight, this accords not only with good law but with common sense. Take Mabel, 98, who has terminal cancer. She is now only two hours from death, and on a ventilator, which she finds increasingly burdensome as death creeps closer. She asks the doctor to remove the ventilator. The doctor agrees on the ground that, although she will die in two hours on the machine and in one hour without it, the machine is merely prolonging the dying process. No sensible doctor would enter 'removal of ventilation' as a cause of death on Mabel's death certificate.

D. A Right to Suicide

The crime of suicide was abolished by the Suicide Act 1961. Since then there has, therefore, been a right to commit suicide. If there is a right to commit suicide, the law cannot sensibly prohibit assisting someone to exercise that right.

i. The Purposes of the Suicide Act

Supporters of this argument could invoke Lord Justice Hoffmann (as he then was), who opined in the *Bland* case that the Suicide Act represented the triumph of the right to self-determination over the sanctity of life. His Lordship was, however, mistaken.

First, conduct which is no longer criminal (or which has never been criminal) may nevertheless be unlawful. It may not be a crime to picnic in your neighbour's garden, or to negligently dent your neighbour's Bentley, but such conduct is nevertheless unlawful and you have no right to engage in it. Suicide has been decriminalised but it has not been made 'lawful'. Secondly, if Parliament intended by the Suicide Act to make suicide 'lawful' or even to create a 'right' to it, why did it make it an offence to assist the exercise of that supposedly 'lawful' conduct or 'right'? From the legislative history of the Suicide Act it is transparent that it was not the intention of Parliament to condone suicide, let alone establish a 'right to suicide'. The minister who guided the legislation through Parliament could hardly have spoken more plainly:

> Because we have taken the view, as Parliament and the Government have taken, that the treatment of people who attempt to commit suicide should no longer be through the criminal courts, it in no way lessens, nor should it lessen, the respect for the sanctity of human life which we all share. It must not be thought that because we are changing the method of treatment for those unfortunate people we seek to depreciate the gravity of the action of anyone who tries to commit suicide.

He added:

> I should like to state as solemnly as I can that it is certainly not the view of the Government, that we wish to give no encouragement whatever to suicide . . . I hope that nothing that I have said will give the impression that the act of self-murder, or self-destruction, is regarded at all lightly by the Home Office or the Government.[36]

As Lord Bingham pointed out in the *Dianne Pretty* case, suicide was decriminalised because the offence was not thought to be a deterrent, because it cast an unwarranted stigma on innocent members of the suicide's family and because it led to the distasteful result of prosecuting attempted suicides. The policy of the law, he noted, remained 'firmly adverse to suicide'.[37]

---

[36] Keown (n 17) 66.
[37] *R (on the application of Pretty) v Director of Public Prosecutions* [2001] UKHL 61 [35].

ii. *The Right to Refuse Treatment: a Shield not a Sword*

Another argument sometimes raised in support of an alleged 'right to suicide' is the English courts' assertion of an apparently absolute right to refuse treatment. If the right to refuse treatment really were absolute, it would include not only refusals which were intended by the patient to avoid treatments which offered no reasonable hope of therapeutic benefit or which involved excessive burdens, but also refusals aimed precisely at ending life, that is, at committing suicide. Imagine Sid, a 25-year-old diabetic and devoted fan of Manchester City. He is in hospital because he fell over and broke his leg while cheering Manchester City against their arch rivals Manchester United. Manchester City lost and were relegated. Relegation spells bankruptcy and the club is to be wound up. Sid is devastated. 'Manchester City is my life', he assures his doctor. 'Life without the club is no longer worth living'. He therefore refuses his next insulin shot so as to put an end to his life. This is plainly a suicidal refusal of treatment. If the courts were to hold that patients have a *right* to commit suicide by refusing treatment and that doctors and nurses might *intentionally* assist or encourage such refusals, the courts would have dug themselves into a hole similar to the one they dug in *Bland*. For the law would then prohibit doctors and nurses from intentionally assisting suicide by an act but would permit them to do so by intentionally withholding or withdrawing life-saving treatment. It is, however, far from clear that the courts have dug themselves into such a hole. Despite their unnecessarily sweeping statements about the right to refuse treatment, the courts have yet to hold that a doctor may, let alone must, withhold or withdraw treatment *with intent to assist* a suicidal refusal of treatment.

First, it appears that the courts have yet to appreciate that a refusal of treatment may be suicidal. They have (like Lord Goff appears to have done in *Bland*) tended to assume that suicide may be committed by an act but not by an omission. However, just as one may commit suicide by jumping in front of a bus, one may do so by failing to jump out of the way of a bus (or by failing to eat, drink, keep warm, etc). The courts have, secondly, yet to decide a case in which the point has been raised and argued before them. In *Re B* a woman with tetraplegia obtained a court order requiring the removal of her life-prolonging ventilation, even though she was not terminally ill and would die as a result of disconnection. The question whether her refusal was suicidal was not considered in the judgment.[38] Thirdly, if the courts were to hold that doctors must withdraw life-prolonging treatment even when the patient's refusal appears suicidally motivated, this would not necessarily endorse a right to suicide or a right to assist suicide. A doctor who withdraws treatment solely in order to respect the patient's legal right to refuse treatment, even if the refusal is suicidal, does not thereby intend to assist suicide. The courts might arguably take the pragmatic line that to require doctors to scrutinise patients' refusals and to force treatment on competent patients if they appear suicidal would be unreasonable, not least given the demands on doctors' time from patients who *want* treatment. Even if the courts were to hold that doctors may intentionally assist or encourage clearly suicidal refusals, this would be no more a reason for allowing active assistance in suicide than *Bland* was for allowing NVAE.

In sum, the courts have held that the right to refuse treatment is a shield against unwanted treatment, not that it is a sword obliging intentional assistance in suicidal refusals.

E. Public Opinion

Opinion polls consistently show that a clear majority of the public supports the decriminalisation of VAE/PAS. The law should reflect public opinion.

This is one of the commonest arguments advanced in favour of decriminalisation. It is also one of the weakest. First, polls about VAE/PAS must be treated with caution. The Mackay Committee commissioned independent research into polls of public and

---

[38] *Re B (Adult: Refusal of Medical Treatment)* [2002] EWHC 429 (Fam).

professional opinion. That research concluded that polls were of 'limited value' and 'could not be accepted at face value as an authentic account' of opinion. This was particularly true of polls of the general public which reflected 'knee-jerk' reactions to simple options and did 'not form a very useful guide to public opinion as support for legislative change'.[39]

Secondly, the mere fact that a majority of the population may support a particular policy hardly makes that policy ethical. Is the ethics of slavery, or torture, or capital punishment to be determined by a show of hands?

F. Legal Failure

The current legal prohibition of VAE/PAS is a failure. Despite the prohibition, they are commonly practised. Decriminalisation would bring them out into the open and permit effective legal regulation.

First, there appears to be little evidence that law against VAE/PAS is frequently broken, let alone that the law is a dead letter. One large-scale survey of US doctors published in 1998 concluded that only 6 per cent had ever performed VAE/PAS. The co-author of the survey concluded: 'This is really not happening very often. That's the most important finding. It's a rare event.'[40] Research in the UK also challenges the claim that doctors commonly break the law. In 2006 Professor Clive Seale published the results of his survey of end-of-life decisions by UK doctors. Seale found that the proportion of deaths from PAS, VAE and NVAE was 'extremely low'.[41] By contrast, as John Griffiths admits, the Dutch rate of euthanasia and physician-assisted suicide is by far the highest in Europe. The comparable rates in 2001–02 between the Netherlands and the UK, expressed as a percentage of all deaths, were:[42]

[39] Mackay (n 18) para 232.
[40] Keown (n 17) 62.
[41] C Seale, 'National Survey of End-of-Life Decisions Made by UK Medical Practitioners' (2006) 20 *Palliative Medicine* 3, 6.
[42] Griffiths et al (n 22) 489 Table 17.2.

– VAE 2.59% vs 0.16%;
– PAS: 0.21% vs 0.00%;
– NVAE: 0.60% vs 0.33%.

A repeat survey of the UK by Seale, published in 2009, concluded: 'Euthanasia, physician-assisted suicide and the ending of life without an explicit patient request . . . are rare or non-existent at both time points'.[43] The second survey also found, as a result of more refined questions, that 'non-treatment decisions' and 'double effect measures' were 'much less common than suggested in earlier estimates, rarely involving intent to end life or being judged to have shortened life by more than a day'.[44] Seale did find a high rate of 'continuous deep sedation' in the UK, but his survey did not ask doctors whether they used it with any intent to hasten death, and he recommends further research into the context in which it is practised. John Griffiths suggests that in the Netherlands there *is* evidence that doctors are using 'terminal sedation' (continuous deep sedation combined with withholding/withdrawing artificially delivered food and fluids) to end life so as to avoid the law's requirements for VAE. Even so, in 2010 the Dutch newspaper *NRC Handelsblad* reported that the number of reported deaths by VAE rose 13 per cent in 2009, to 2636, following an increase of 10 per cent in 2008, and that the 2008 increase had prompted the health ministry to set up an investigation.

There is, then, scant evidence to support the argument that VAE/PAS and NVAE are common in the UK or US. Moreover, casting doubt on the claim that decriminalisation brings transparency and control, we shall see that Dutch doctors have flouted their legal guidelines for VAE/PAS in thousands of cases. Further, Griffiths suggests a sizeable incidence of illicit assistance in suicide in the Netherlands by doctors *and* laypeople. He cites research by Dr Chabot suggesting that some 1600 people per year have committed assisted suicide outwith the legal guidelines by

---

[43] C Seale, 'End-of-Life Decisions in the UK Involving Medical Practitioners' (2009) 23 *Palliative Medicine* 198, 201.

[44] ibid 198.

taking sleeping pills which were supplied by a doctor or prepared for ingestion by a layperson, or both. Griffiths observes that many serious crimes are therefore involved over which control is essentially non-existent.

That the incidence of VAE/PAS should increase with decriminalisation accords with common sense. Dr Neil Gorsuch, author of a leading treatise on VAE/PAS and now a judge on the US Federal Court of Appeals, has pointed out that such an increase also accords with the 'law of demand' which holds that, other things being equal, the quantity demanded of a good falls as its cost rises. He explains:

> Consistent with the law of demand, one would expect that if certain 'costs' associated with assisted suicide and euthanasia (for example, the social stigma and difficulty of finding a willing physician to help when the practices remain illegal) are lowered or eliminated by legalization, *more*, not fewer, people would take advantage of this fact and seek an early death.[45]

In relation to the decriminalisation of abortion, the statistical evidence seems consistent with the law of demand. According to data cited by the pro-choice Alan Guttmacher Institute in the US, by 1993, 20 years after the Supreme Court struck down all laws against abortion, the number of abortions had doubled to 1.5 million per year, and by 2008 almost 50 million had been performed.[46] In England and Wales, the number of notified abortions rose from 24,000 in 1968 (the Abortion Act 1967 came into effect on 27 April that year) to over 180,000 in 1989.[47] Even an ardent pro-choice advocate might hesitate to claim that the increase was merely a translation of previously illegal abortions to legal abortions. Professor Glanville Williams, who was such an advocate, wrote that the decriminalisation of abortion produced

---

[45] NM Gorsuch, *The Future of Assisted Suicide and Euthanasia* (Princeton, Princeton University Press, 2006) 133.

[46] www.guttmacher.org/pubs/journals/4304111.pdf Table 1.

[47] http://www.dh.gov.uk/prod_consum_dh/groups/dh_digitalassets/documents/digitalasset/dh_116336.pdf Table 1.

an 'entirely new clientele', and that its effect was 'to add the total of legal abortions to the total of illegal abortions rather than to reduce the number of illegal abortions'.[48] Why would it be any different with the decriminalisation of VAE/PAS?

Secondly, even if VAE/PAS *were* frequently performed in countries where it is illegal, would this amount to a cogent argument for its decriminalisation? For all we know, female genital mutilation is frequently practised by disreputable doctors in the UK. Would this justify its decriminalisation? Perjury may also be frequent. Speeding is very frequent. Is frequency not a reason for more effective enforcement rather than for decriminalisation? Moreover, whatever the incidence of illegal VAE/PAS in the UK and the US, the laws against them are clearly a long way from laws like Prohibition which have not only failed to eliminate the proscribed conduct, but have been so widely and publicly flouted by respectable members of society as to lose 'even the character of symbolising a real societal commitment to the values they purport to uphold'.[49]

Thirdly, *would* decriminalisation of VAE/PAS bring whatever illegal practice there may be 'out into the open'? Why should we assume that any doctors who are currently willing to commit the crime of murder and/or assisting suicide would be willing to comply with guidelines for VAE/PAS? A few jurisdictions now permit VAE/PAS. The most important of these are the Netherlands, which has by far the longest experience of decriminalisation, and Oregon, whose law is now held up as a model which should be followed across the US and in the UK. Let us now consider whether the bold claims made on their behalf withstand scrutiny.

---

[48] See J Keown and D Jones, 'Surveying the Foundations of Medical Law' (2008) 16(1) *Medical Law Review* 85, 118fns 187–88.
[49] J Finnis, 'Abortion and Legal Rationality' (1970) 3 *Adelaide Law Review* 431, 436.

G. The Netherlands

The Dutch experience confirms that VAE/PAS can be brought out into the open and subjected to effective control. The Dutch law contains strict safeguards which have prevented abuse and any slide down the 'slippery slope'.

Dutch law has permitted VAE/PAS since a decision of the Dutch Supreme Court in 1984. The Court held that a doctor may claim the defence of 'necessity' in cases where, according to 'responsible medical opinion', the duty to alleviate suffering overrides the duty not to kill. Shortly after the decision, the Royal Dutch Medical Association issued guidelines for doctors. In 2002 the Termination of Life on Request and Assisted Suicide (Review Procedures) Act came into force. The Act in essence enshrines the guidelines in statutory form. Inter alia, the Act requires that the patient made a 'voluntary and carefully considered' request (often described as an 'explicit request') for VAE/PAS; that the patient was experiencing 'unbearable suffering with no prospect of improvement'; and that before carrying out VAE/PAS the doctor consulted with an independent doctor and, afterwards, reported the case to the local medical examiner. The report is then to be forwarded by the examiner to a Regional Review Committee

Defenders of the Dutch experience (not least the Dutch) claim that it shows that VAE/PAS can be effectively controlled. This claim, however, is not borne out by the empirical evidence. Much of this evidence has been helpfully generated by the Dutch themselves in the form of government-sponsored national surveys into end-of-life medical practice in 1990, 1995, 2001 and 2005. In what follows, we shall rely largely on the evidence as it is set out in the work of Professor John Griffiths, an informed defender of the Dutch experience.

i. Voluntary Request

In the Netherlands, 87 per cent of cases of VAE/PAS are performed by GPs. Only 3 per cent of patients are referred for psychiatric evaluation. In light of the concerns raised by the Royal College of Psychiatrists,[50] there must be doubt about how voluntary and informed were the requests made by the remaining 97 per cent. Moreover, a Dutch survey of cancer patients found, to the surprise of the researchers, not only that depressed patients are more than four times as likely to request euthanasia (no fewer than 44 per cent of the depressed patients surveyed requested euthanasia), but that there was no significant association between depression and prognosis: it was the depressed patients, not the sickest patients, who seemed to be requesting euthanasia.

No less doubt must attach to any requests for euthanasia made in 'advance directives' by patients who are now incompetent. Griffiths points out that advance requests made in writing by those over 16 are valid. He writes that there must be no doubt about the authenticity of the document, the competence of the author and the voluntariness of its execution. But he also points out that there are no formal requirements for advance directives in Dutch law, such as witnesses or regular renewal. How, then, can a doctor faced with a slip of paper requesting VAE, allegedly typed perhaps many years before by the now incompetent patient whom the doctor may never have met, know that these conditions have been satisfied? Griffiths notes that patients' families are sometimes suspected of putting the patient (or the doctor) under pressure. The lax Dutch law relating to advance directives would appear to give impatient relatives an alternative to pressuring the doctor: simply type a note purporting to be a request for euthanasia by the patient. Moreover, Dutch law also allows children as young as 16 to access VAE/PAS – even children as young as 12, if their request is supported by their parents or a guardian. Doubt must surely surround the competence of children to make such a request.

Apart from the many cases raising doubts about how autonomous the request for VAE/PAS was, there have been many cases in which Dutch doctors have admitted that there was no

---

[50] Noted above, pp 97–98.

explicit request at all. In the 1980s the Dutch claimed that patients' lives would be ended only at their explicit request. For example Professor Henk Leenen, an architect of Dutch euthanasia, wrote that without a request, euthanasia was murder and breached Article 2 of the European Convention. The Board of the Dutch Society for Voluntary Euthanasia agreed that NVAE was murder and claimed that it would be prosecuted and sentenced as such. That was then. The Dutch data have disclosed that medical murder is not uncommon and is rarely prosecuted. The first Dutch survey revealed that in 1990 there were 2300 cases of VAE and 400 cases of PAS. (These figures are conservative: they omit many other cases in which doctors admitted conduct, active and well as passive, in which their primary intention was to end life.) Remarkably, the survey also revealed that a further 1000 patients (most of whom were incompetent, but 140 of whom were wholly competent and a further 110 partly competent) had been given a lethal injection without having made an explicit request. (By 2005 the number had halved, but each case remains, in Dutch law, murder.) Commenting on these 1000 cases the New York State Task Force observed:

> If euthanasia were practiced in a comparable percentage of cases in the United States, voluntary euthanasia would account for 36,000 deaths each year, and euthanasia without the patient's consent would occur in an additional 16,000 deaths . . . The Task Force members regard this risk as unacceptable.[51]

Dutch law may even be moving to permit such cases of NVAE. In one case the defendant physician, Dr van Oijen, was convicted of murdering a woman who was not suffering unbearably and who had made it clear she did not want to die, a fact which made the case closer to IVAE than NVAE. (Reflecting the extreme leniency of the Dutch courts, his sentence was one week's imprisonment, suspended for two years.) Professor Griffiths observes: 'the Supreme Court ruled that the justification of necessity in

---

[51] New York State Task Force (n 8) 134.

principle can be available in a case of ending the life of a dying patient without the patient's request'.[52] He writes:

> If one may venture a prediction, it would be this: the idea of an 'inhumane death' will, in one form or another, come increasingly to be accepted not only as a legitimate (prospective) reason for requesting euthanasia but as a justification for 'help in dying' [NVAE].[53]

He adds:

> In short, there seems to be a subtle addition to the existing grounds for the justification of termination of life going on: not only the patient's subjective experience of suffering, but also the idea in the eyes of intimate beholders that such a death is something one should not let happen to a human being, can suffice.[54]

He also notes that Dutch Courts of Appeal have already endorsed NVAE in the case of disabled babies. Pediatricians have since drawn up guidelines, notably the 'Groningen Protocol', for infanticide. Griffiths reasonably suggests, in light of these developments, that Dutch law is slowly but steadily moving in the direction of explicit recognition of a doctor's duty to ensure that his patient dies a 'humane' or 'dignified' death.[55] The ease with which such an arbitrary notion could be extended to vulnerable groups, including the frail elderly, the demented and the disabled, scarcely needs emphasis.

Yet further evidence of the growing acceptance of NVAE is the striking statement by the lead authors of the Dutch national surveys that it is now the responsibility of *patients* to make it clear, when competent, if they do *not* want to be given a lethal injection should they become incompetent. As translated by Dr Fenigsen:

> [I]t is the patient who is now responsible in the Netherlands for avoiding termination of his life; if he does not wish to be killed by his doctor then he must state it clearly orally and in writing, well in advance.[56]

---

[52] Griffiths et al (n 22) 41, citing *Nederlandse Jurisprudentie* 2005, no 217: 9.
[53] Griffiths et al (n 22) 73.
[54] ibid 142.
[55] ibid 143.
[56] J Keown, *Considering Physician-Assisted Suicide* (London, Carenotkilling, 2006) 6.

We mentioned above that VAE/PAS advocates claim that Dutch doctors are trusted by their patients. However, one wonders just how many Dutch patients who still trust that their doctors will not kill them without request are aware of the incidence of NVAE and of the fact that it is now up to them to make it clear if they do not want it? Professor Leenen wrote that patients' trust would not diminish if they were sure that they would not be killed without request. But how sure can Dutch patients now be? Emily Jackson takes at face value assurances by Dutch doctors about how conscientiously they follow the guidelines, quoting for example the claim by a Dutch doctor that euthanasia is only permitted 'within a meaningful relationship'[57] (whatever that means): where is such a requirement in Dutch Law? She does not consider that such trust as Dutch patients have in their doctors might be as misplaced as the trust that Dr Shipman's patients had in him. She claims that Shipman's breach of trust occurred in a country where euthanasia is illegal, 'so we cannot plausibly argue that the illegality of euthanasia is necessary to prevent murderously inclined doctors from killing their patients'.[58] The fact that laws are broken hardly makes it implausible to argue that they are necessary.

ii. 'Unbearable Suffering with No Prospect of Improvement'

The requirement of 'unbearable suffering' has proved elastic. First, provided that a patient's assertion that suffering is unbearable is 'understandable' to a normal doctor and provided it is due to a recognised medical disorder, it is largely a matter of a patient's subjective feeling. Secondly, the suffering need not arise from a terminal or even a somatic illness. This was so held by the Dutch Supreme Court in the *Chabot* case,[59] where psychiatrist Dr Chabot helped a woman to kill herself solely because of her grief at the death of her two sons. Thirdly, fear of future dementia can qualify, even though the patient will not suffer at all when demented.

---

[57] Jackson, 'Death, Euthanasia and the Medical Profession' (n 1) 40.
[58] ibid 51.
[59] *Nederlandse Jurisprudentie* 1994, no 656.

And, if fear of dementia, why not fear of physical deterioration or dependency? Fourthly, although the Supreme Court in the *Brongersma* case[60] ruled out existential suffering or 'tiredness of life', on the ground that the suffering must be predominantly due to a medically classified disease or disorder if a doctor is to be acting within the scope of professional competence, it is doubtful whether this limitation will stand. An advisory committee of the Royal Dutch Medical Association has since concluded that euthanasia for existential suffering should be permitted. It is not difficult to see why. If it is not outside a doctor's competence to make the moral judgment that death would benefit the patient because of physical or mental suffering, why should it be any different in relation to existential suffering, even assuming a clear line can be drawn between the two types of suffering? Griffiths points out that even after *Brongersma*, uncertainty remains and that doctors in such cases might simply report the patient's disease or disorder as the source of the suffering. Finally, as regards the requirement that there be 'no prospect of improvement', this can be satisfied even if there is a viable alternative which is refused by the patient, provided the doctor regards the refusal as 'understandable' (and at least if the illness is somatic).

A disturbing illustration of how sweepingly 'unbearable suffering' and 'voluntary and carefully considered request' can be interpreted in practice has been provided by a leading Dutch practitioner of euthanasia. When asked if he would rule out euthanasia for a patient who said he wanted to die because he felt a nuisance to his children, who wanted him dead so that they could inherit his estate, the doctor replied:

> I . . . think in the end I wouldn't, because that kind of influence – these children wanting the money now – is the same kind of power from the past that . . . shaped us all. The same thing goes for religion . . . education . . . the kind of family he was raised in, all kinds of influences from the past that we can't put aside.[61]

---

[60] *Nederlandse Jurisprudentie* 2003, no 167.
[61] Dr H Cohen, interviewed by the author on 26 July 1989. Keown (n 17) 87.

iii. Reporting

The four national surveys have shown that in thousands of cases doctors have flouted the legal requirement to report. In 1990 the rate of non-reporting was 80 per cent. By 2005 it had fallen, but was still running at 20 per cent. Each failure to report not only breaches the guidelines but also involves the criminal offence of falsifying a death certificate by entering death by 'natural causes'.

iv. Critics

It is not surprising, in view of the above evidence, that the Dutch experience has drawn criticisms from many quarters, including the UN Committee on Human Rights. In 2001 the Committee ventilated several concerns, not least the NVAE of disabled babies. In 2009 the Committee reiterated concerns, not only 'at the extent of euthanasia and assisted suicides' but also that a physician can terminate a patient's life 'without any independent review by a judge or magistrate to guarantee that this decision was not the subject of undue influence or misapprehension'.[62] It recommended that the Dutch legislation be reviewed in light of the UN's recognition of the right to life.

Critics include those who support VAE/PAS in principle. In 1998 Griffiths et al, having noted the 'intrinsic ineffectiveness of control based on self-reporting', observed that the control regime did not provide 'effective control', that the results of the first two national surveys which had by then been published had been 'pretty devastating' and that the regime seemed 'all bark and no bite'.[63] However, in their more recent book published in 2008, Griffiths et al assert that there is now a:

> well-developed system of control, consisting of expert consultation before euthanasia is carried out and assessment afterwards by the

---

[62] UN Human Rights Committee, 'Consideration of Reports Submitted by States Parties Under Article 40 of the Covenant' CCPR/C/NLD/CO/4 (25 August 2009) para 7 www.unhcr.org/refworld/publisher,HRC,,,4aa7aa642,0.html.

[63] J Griffiths et al, *Euthanasia and Law in the Netherlands* (Amsterdam, Amsterdam University Press, 1998) 257–68.

Regional Review Committees, which have been designed to be acceptable to doctors.[64]

This about-face, which appears to rest on improvements in consultation and reporting, is puzzling. First: consultation. The more recent book points out that in 1999 a national programme (SCEN: 'Support and Consultation Euthanasia Netherlands') was instituted under which doctors could be trained in the medical, ethical and legal aspects of euthanasia consultation and that now in 90 per cent of reported cases doctors have consulted a SCEN physician. However, while this belated training programme may well have improved the quality of the consultation process in many cases, the requirement of consultation with an independent doctor is nothing new. Moreover, even consulting a doctor who has undergone an SCEN training course (and consultation with such a doctor is not legally required) is some way from consulting a specialist in psychiatry or palliative care. As we noted above, most cases of euthanasia (87 per cent) are dealt with by GPs, and only 3 per cent of euthanasia patients are referred to a psychiatrist. Dr van Oijen, the doctor convicted of murdering a patient against her express wish, was himself a SCEN consultant. Further, a consultant's failure to see the patient, a negative opinion by a consultant, or a failure to consult an independent consultant, will not necessarily trigger prosecution. Although the legislation requires consultation, the book points out that the Review Committees interpret this in a 'flexible way', thereby correcting what it (oddly) describes as a 'legislative mistake'.[65]

Secondly: reporting. The book invokes the introduction of Review Committees in 1998 – which replaced prosecutors as the destination for physicians' reports – and the subsequent improvement in the reporting rate from 20 per cent to 80 per cent. It contends that one of the most important advantages of these committees is that their decision-making is more transparent than the previous prosecutorial review system. But greater

---

[64]   Griffiths et al (n 22) 49.
[65]   ibid 84, fn 139.

openness about consideration of the reports has no bearing on the reliability of those reports. The system of review still relies on self-reporting, the 'intrinsic ineffectiveness' of which was rightly criticised in the previous book. Not surprisingly, the committees, staffed by three active professionals who mostly do their committee work 'on the side' and whose secretaries are 'overburdened',[66] 'very rarely' find that the doctor has breached the requirements and refer the case to the prosecutors. Most reports received by the committees are 'unproblematic' and 'hardly afford anything to discuss'. Moreover, the committees find that doctors acted properly even when their actions 'were not entirely in conformity with the legal requirements'. Of the few cases which they have referred to prosecutors, none has resulted in prosecution. The prosecutors themselves 'hardly ever bring criminal charges in the tiny fraction of all cases that do come to their attention'. The 'handful' of prosecutions in recent years are of non-reported cases which 'happen accidentally' to come to prosecutorial attention. And there are many unreported cases. For example, the more recent book admits that although there are known to be 'a considerable number' of cases of NVAE, 'hardly any' have been reported.[67] In relation to the NVAE of infants it states that 'control over termination of life of severely defective newborn babies cannot yet be regarded as legally adequate' and 'because of an apparently low reporting rate, it is certainly not effective'.[68] How can a system of review by part-timers who rely on what they are told by those who report, and who are not told anything by those who do not, sensibly be described as a 'well-developed system of control'? As Judge Gorsuch has asked of the Dutch regime:

> Does a regime dependent on self-reporting by physicians who have no interest in recording any case falling outside the guidelines

---

[66] M Cook, 'Steep Rise in Official Dutch Euthanasia' www.mercatornet.com/careful/view/8312/.
[67] Griffiths et al (n 22) 127–45.
[68] ibid 252.

adequately protect against lives taken erroneously, mistakenly, or as a result of abuse or coercion? How would we ever know?[69]

We will recall that Griffiths suggests that to encourage doctors to report NVAE, it should be reclassified as 'normal medical practice'. Gorsuch notes that, curiously, Griffiths does not give any significant consideration to the question whether allowing doctors to kill patients without consent might also lead to additional cases of abusive, coercive, and mistaken killings, and that Griffiths' proposal would appear to rule out prosecution, whether the doctor's motives were compassionate or cruel. Gorsuch adds:

> In Griffiths' preferred regime, only professional and civil sanctions would be available as remedies when doctors kill without consent – and even these remedies would be available only if and when doctors kill in the absence of what he calls 'normal medical practice' – although Griffiths fails to specify when he thinks killing a patient without consent should be considered 'normal'.[70]

Judge Gorsuch also points out that there is no guarantee that decriminalisation of NVAE would increase reporting: doctors might still be deterred from reporting by possible civil and professional sanctions. In short, Griffiths exaggerates the significance of changes which do little to ensure that the guidelines are satisfied in any given case, to meet the serious concerns which have been voiced by critics like the UN Human Rights Committee, or to remedy (in his own words) the 'intrinsic ineffectiveness' of a system based on self-reporting. It all seems more a case of plus ça change . . .

In 2004 Raphael Cohen-Almagor, a supporter of VAE/PAS who has conducted empirical research in the Netherlands, concluded that the Dutch regime suffers from serious flaws, that all of the guidelines are regularly broken, and that the Dutch tend to condone NVAE. The high number of unreported cases, and the

[69] Gorsuch (n 45) 114.
[70] ibid 115.

fact that many physicians did not wish to be bothered with the procedures, was, he found, 'alarming'.[71]

Finally, we will recall the observation in 2009 by Dr Borst, a key architect of Dutch euthanasia, that legalised euthanasia had been followed by decline in the quality of care for the terminally ill and by Dr The that many patients asked to die 'out of fear' because of poor palliative care. Dr Borst also commented that euthanasia had been legalised 'far too early', adding: 'In the Netherlands, we first listened to the political and societal demand in favour of euthanasia. Obviously this was not in the proper order.'[72]

So much, then, for claims that the Dutch have subjected VAE/PAS to effective control. The evidence generated by the Dutch themselves discloses widespread breach of the guidelines, with virtual impunity.

H. Oregon

The experience of Oregon's Death With Dignity Act (DWDA) is reassuring. The law contains strict safeguards against abuse. Moreover, the number of cases reported by doctors to the relevant authority (the Oregon Department of Public Health – ODPH) has been very low and there is no evidence of abuse in practice.

i. The Law: 'Strict Safeguards'?

The DWDA, which came into force in 1997, provides inter alia:

> An adult who is capable, is a resident of Oregon, and has been determined by the attending physician and consulting physician to be suffering from a terminal disease, and who has voluntarily expressed his or her wish to die, may make a written request for medication for the purpose of ending his or her life in a humane and dignified manner.[73]

---

[71] R Cohen-Almagor, *Euthanasia in the Netherlands* (Dordrecht, Kluwer Academic Publishers, 2004) 175–79.

[72] See text at n 27 above.

[73] Keown (n 17) 167.

How 'strict' are the Act's 'safeguards' against abuse? Health law expert Professor Alexander Capron has concluded they are 'largely illusory'.[74] His assessment is, as we shall see, sound.

The Act requires:

(i) the involvement of two physicians; that the patient be referred for counsel-ling if either physician thinks the patient may be psychologically disordered, and that the attending physician inform the patient about alternatives includ-ing pain control.

Neither of the physicians need be the patient's regular physician and, if they are not, neither need consult the patient's regular physician. There is nothing to stop the patient 'shopping around' to find two compliant physicians. Nor need the two physicians be independent. Neither physician need have any expertise in psychiatry. How, then, can the Act ensure that requests for PAS are not a symptom of a treatable mental illness? Nor is there any-thing in the Act to ensure that when the patient swallows the lethal drugs, which may be months after obtaining the prescrip-tion, the patient is not *then* suffering from a psychiatric or psycho-logical disorder impairing their judgment. The Act does little, therefore, to address the concerns of the Royal College of Psychiatrists noted earlier.[75] Judge Gorsuch notes that when the state of Oregon wishes to confine for a maximum of five days a patient with suicidal impulses, the patient is entitled to an exami-nation by a mental health expert. 'How', he asks trenchantly 'can one coherently explain and defend a regulatory regime that affords terminally ill patients less protection against the possibil-ity of a mistaken death due to a psychiatric ailment than it affords all patients against the possibility of a mistaken five-day confine-ment from the same cause?'[76]

As for palliative care, the Act requires the attending physician to inform the patient of feasible alternatives, including hospice care and pain control. But neither doctor need have any expertise

---

[74] ibid 180.
[75] See pp 97–98.
[76] Gorsuch (n 45) 179.

in palliative care. If the doctors lack such expertise, how informed can the patient be? Further, being informed about palliative care may be quite different from experiencing its benefits. The ODPH, in concluding that patients who were assisted in suicide in Oregon were receiving adequate end-of-life care, observed that a high percentage had advance directives and were enrolled in hospice care. However, 'hospice care' in Oregon may simply mean domiciliary visits and, as Professor Kathleen Foley, a palliative care expert, and Professor Herbert Hendin, a psychiatrist and expert in suicide prevention, have commented: 'neither advance directives nor enrollment in a hospice program, any more than admission to a hospital, are proof of adequate care'.[77] Finally, the Act gives the physicians complete immunity – criminal, civil and professional – provided they act in 'good faith'. It apparently protects even grossly negligent diagnosis, prognosis and evaluation of competence.

(ii)   that the patient make an oral request for PAS, reiterated in no less than 15 days, and a written request which must be witnessed; that no less than 48 hours elapse between the written request and the writing of the prescription; and that the attending physician file a report with the ODPH.

The waiting period, while better than none, is hardly adequate to ensure that the request is truly voluntary. And the requirement that two witnesses attest that to the best of their knowledge the patient is capable, acting voluntarily, and not coerced, could be satisfied by two strangers invited in off the street. As for the requirement on the attending physician to file a report with the ODPH, there is no guarantee that all doctors file reports or that the reports they file are accurate. The ODPH itself has admitted that it is not an investigatory agency, that it cannot know the extent to which PAS is practised outside the DWDA, and that the reports which are filed could be completely unreliable. As Gorsuch points out:

---

[77] (2000) 30(1) *Hastings Center Report* (letters) 5.

even if a doctor were actually to take the extraordinary step of reporting himself or herself as having violated the law, Oregon's statute imposes no duty on the health division to investigate or pursue such cases, let alone root them out in the absence of any such self-reports.[78]

There is no guarantee, therefore, that the low incidence of PAS indicated by the ODPH's annual statistical reports is accurate, or that the law is being observed in practice. Daniel Callahan has described the Oregon regulations as 'a Potemkin-village form of regulatory obfuscation. They look good, sound good, feel good, but have nothing behind them'.[79]

(iii) that the patient has a 'terminal disease' and may be given a lethal prescription but not a lethal injection.

Although the Oregon law is laxer than the Dutch law in not requiring that the patient be suffering (unbearably or otherwise), it is tighter in that it does not allow VAE, and is limited to cases of 'terminal disease'. However, these limitations resist clear definition. The distinction between VAE and PAS is not always clear-cut and 'terminal disease' is easy neither to define nor to predict. The Libyan 'Lockerbie bomber', Abdelbaset al-Megrahi, was released from a Scottish prison in 2009 because he was diagnosed with terminal prostate cancer and given about three months to live. As of 2011 he is still alive. Moreover, these limitations are unlikely to stand. Once one accepts PAS for the 'terminally ill', why discriminate against the chronically ill, who have longer to suffer? If the law allows PAS out of respect for patient choice, why should it deny a patient's preference for VAE, particularly if the patient is unable to commit suicide? Could this limitation withstand a court challenge that it discriminates against those whose disability prevents them from committing suicide? Moreover, Dutch doctors have noted that a law which permits only PAS will fail, in a significant proportion of cases, to ensure a

---

[78] Gorsuch (n 45) 118–19.
[79] D Callahan, 'Organized Obfuscation: Advocacy for Physician-Assisted Suicide' (2008) 38(5) *Hastings Center Report* 30, 32.

quick and painless death. Cases in the Netherlands which start out as PAS not uncommonly end as VAE. One leading Dutch euthanasia expert has commented:

> Thinking that physician-assisted suicide is the entire answer to the question of ending of life of a suffering patient . . . is a fantasy. There will always be patients who cannot drink, or are semiconscious, or prefer that a physician perform this act. Experience has taught us that there are many cases of assisted suicide in which the suicide fails. Physicians need to be aware of the necessity to intervene before patients awaken.[80]

One Dutch study reported that around 20 per cent of cases in which the doctor intended to assist suicide ended up with the doctor administering a lethal injection in order to overcome complications. In view of all this, expert bodies like the Walton Committee have been right to conclude that PAS does not raise significantly different issues from VAE.

ii.   No Abuse?

The annual statistical reports issued by the ODPH indicate that relatively few patients have availed themselves of the Act since it came into force in late 1997. The latest report, for 2010, indicates that from 1998 to 2010 only 525 patients have used the law to commit suicide. The trend of reported cases has, however, been upward, from 16 in 1998 to 65 in 2010, and there is of course no guarantee that all cases have been reported.

Daniel Callahan has noted that the assurances from Oregon that there is no abuse are, in their confidence and firmness, 'the equal of those expressed in the Netherlands prior to its confidential surveys'.[81] Moreover, the legal regime in Oregon is not *designed* to detect abuse: PAS is practised under a carapace of legal confidentiality. This renders claims about lack of abuse little more than

---

[80] GK Kimsma, 'Euthanasia Drugs in the Netherlands' in DC Thomasma et al (eds), *Asking to Die: Inside the Dutch Debate about Euthanasia* (Dordrecht, Kluwer, 1998) 135, 142–43.

[81] Callahan (n 79) 32.

assertion. The Oregon law relies essentially on the competence and honesty of participating doctors and, as in the Netherlands, doctors who have ignored the law are unlikely to report their non-compliance or to be detected if they fail to report. As Judge Gorsuch puts it: 'Oregon's regulations are crafted in ways that make reliable and relevant data and case descriptions difficult to obtain'.[82]

Even the relatively meagre data which is collated by the ODPH, and which give us little insight into each individual case, raise a number of serious concerns. They show that as in the Netherlands, the vast majority of patients (92.5 per cent) have not been referred for psychiatric or psychological evaluation. A survey by Ganzini et al revealed that three of 18 patients given lethal prescriptions had treatable but undiagnosed depression at the time and went on to commit suicide. She concluded: 'the current practice of the Death with Dignity Act may fail to protect some patients whose choices are influenced by depression'.[83] Even in relation to the tiny minority who have been referred for psychological evaluation, it is relevant to note that another survey by Ganzini found that only 6 per cent of Oregon psychiatrists were very confident that they could determine competence in a single visit, in the absence of a long-term relationship with the patient.[84] Moreover, the ODPH reports also show that one in five patients (21.3 per cent) has expressed concern about inadequate pain control and more than one in three patients (35.3 per cent) a concern about being a burden on family, friends or caregivers. The three most common reasons for seeking a lethal prescription have been 'losing autonomy' (91.2 per cent), a decreasing ability 'to engage in activities making life enjoyable' (88.1 per cent) and 'loss of dignity' (84.1 per cent). These reasons are some distance from the sort of 'hard cases' of 'unbearable suffering' standardly used to

---

[82] Gorsuch (n 45) 119.

[83] L Ganzini et al, 'Prevalence of Depression and Anxiety in Patients Requesting Physicians' Aid in Dying: Cross-Sectional Survey' (2008) 337 *British Medical Journal* 1682.

[84] L Ganzini et al, 'Attitudes of Oregon Psychiatrists toward Physician-Assisted Suicide' (1996) 153 *American Journal of Psychiatry* 1469, 1474.

illustrate the alleged need for VAE/PAS. Further, the majority of patients have been guided through the DWDA process by members of the pressure group which promoted the legislation, 'Compassion & Choices'.

Absence of evidence of abuse is not evidence of absence of abuse. Moreover, despite the iron screen of secrecy surrounding PAS in Oregon, a number of disturbing cases have come to light. One concerned Kate Cheney, an 85-year-old widow with terminal stomach cancer. Kate, accompanied by her daughter Erika, who had moved from Arizona to care for her, went to request assistance in suicide from her physician at her Health Maintenance Organisation (HMO), Kaiser Permanente. Erika described this doctor as 'dismissive' and obtained a referral to another doctor at Kaiser. This doctor arranged a psychiatric examination for Kate. The psychiatrist concluded that Kate did not seem to be explicitly pushing for assisted suicide, that she lacked the high degree of capacity necessary to weigh options about it, and noted that although Kate seemed to accept this assessment, Erika became very angry. Kaiser then suggested another assessment by an outside consultant. This consultant concluded that Kate was able to decide, although her choices might have been influenced by her family and that Erika might have been 'somewhat coercive'. Kate received a prescription for lethal drugs and subsequently took them. Judge Gorsuch comments that such cases:

> encapsulate and illustrate some of the difficult questions about Oregon's assisted suicide regime alluded to by the [Oregon] data . . .: what role is depression, as opposed to terminal illness, actually playing in patient decisions to die in Oregon? Are alternative options, including treatment for depression, being fully presented (or presented at all)? Are the doctors that prescribe death even knowledgeable about the alternatives that exist? To what extent are family members unduly influencing patient choices and physician evaluations? What would have happened if family members in each case had argued *against* the request to die and offered care? Should patients be allowed to 'shop' around for physicians and psychologists who will find them competent? Do psychologists and physicians have an

obligation to do more than a cursory examination? Should they consult the patient's primary care providers and other doctors or psychologists who may have refused prior requests for lethal medication by the patient? Would Cheney's HMO have offered to pay for a second opinion if the first psychiatrist had found Cheney competent? Do HMOs have a conflict of interest – given that assisted suicide is unquestionably cheaper than continuing care – that may provide an incentive for them to encourage patients to seek death?[85]

Disturbingly, Oregon patients have now received letters from the state informing them that, although it will not fund certain life-prolonging drugs, it will pay for PAS.

A paper by Battin et al in 2007 claimed that, statistically, there is no evidence from Oregon or the Netherlands that decriminalisation has had a disproportionate impact on vulnerable groups. However, to show that the proportion from these groups who accessed VAE/PAS is statistically similar to the proportion who died naturally is not to show that their vulnerability was not exploited, or that their deaths were not the result of malice or mistake. Moreover, Baroness Finlay and Dr Rob George have responded that the notion of 'vulnerability' used by Battin et al is problematic; that subsequent Oregon data show that PAS *is* in fact more common among the elderly (the median age being over 70), and that later research by Ganzini[86] has shown that some patients approved for PAS were suffering from undiagnosed depression. In a critical overview of the DWDA published in 2008, Professors Hendin and Foley conclude that Oregon physicians appear to have been given great power without being in a position to exercise it responsibly:

> They are expected to inform patients that alternatives are possible without being required to be knowledgeable about such alternatives or to consult someone who is. They are expected to evaluate patient decision-making capacity and judgment without a requirement for psychiatric expertise or consultation. They are expected to make

---

[85] Gorsuch (n 45) 125.
[86] See text at fn83.

decisions about voluntariness without having to see those close to the patient who may exert a variety of pressures, from subtle to coercive.

Hendin and Foley add:

> They are expected to do all of this without necessarily knowing the patient for more than fifteen days. Since physicians cannot be held responsible for wrongful deaths if they have acted in good faith, substandard medical practice is permitted, physicians are protected from the consequences, and patients are left unprotected while believing they have acquired a new right.[87]

Finally, even if the DWDA *were* working well in Oregon, a sparsely populated and affluent state, it does not follow that it would work well in other, more densely populated and less affluent US states, or in the UK. Small wonder that, while neighbouring Washington state has voted to follow Oregon, many other US states have voted not to.

I. Religion

It is commonly argued that opposition to VAE/PAS is essentially 'religious' and that in secular, pluralistic societies religious voices should be disqualified from the political debate. During the debate on the Joffe Bill one journalist wrote an article entitled: 'I'd like to die with dignity and I don't want the medieval brigade interfering'. She argued that while religious believers were entitled to reject suicide for themselves, they were not entitled to impose pain on others. The Joffe debate, she claimed, pitched 'the medieval forces of religion against the modern forces of freedom'.[88] Similarly, a later article, by Simon Jenkins, was entitled: 'Denial of the right to die is sheer religious primitivism'. That the law was

---

[87] H Hendin and K Foley, 'Physician-Assisted Suicide in Oregon: A Medical Perspective' (2008) 106 *Michigan Law Review* 1613, 1639.

[88] C Cavendish, 'I'd Like to Die with Dignity and I Don't Want the Medieval Brigade Interfering' *The Times* (11 May 2006).

supported by the Archbishops of Canterbury and Westminster and the Chief Rabbi was, he wrote, 'astonishing', and their opposition to change would come to be seen as 'not just illiberal but cruel'.[89]

It is surprising that anyone should think that opposition to VAE/PAS is essentially religious. First, while it is true that the great religions including Judaism, Christianity and (oddly omitted from Jenkins' list) Islam, have long been opposed to VAE/PAS, opposition has also been voiced (as we have noted above) by many secular bodies including the Walton Committee, the New York State Task Force, the Royal College of Physicians and the World Medical Association. One need not be religious to believe either that legalising VAE/PAS would breach the right to life (the 'cornerstone of law and of social relationships', as the Walton Committee aptly described it) or that it would threaten the vulnerable or lead to NVAE. Indeed, one the of earliest and most powerful arguments against legalisation was (and remains) Professor Yale Kamisar's classic article, 'Some Non-Religious Views Against Proposed "Mercy Killing" Legislation'.[90] Secondly, while many secular bodies oppose VAE/PAS, not all religious believers do. In the House of Lords' debate on the Joffe Bill religious believers spoke on both sides. Thirdly, even religious voices against VAE/PAS do not necessarily rest their opposition on theological grounds. For example, in his speech in the House of Lords against the Joffe Bill the Archbishop of Canterbury invoked the logical slippery slope, not God. Finally, shouldn't pluralism cut both ways? Should campaigns in defence of human rights, such as William Wilberforce's campaign against slavery or the Reverend Martin Luther King's crusade for civil rights, be disqualified if they are motivated by and grounded in the belief that we are all 'created equal'?

---

[89] S Jenkins, 'Denial of the Right to Die is Sheer Religious Primitivism' *The Guardian* (22 October 2008).

[90] Y Kamisar, 'Some Non-Religious Views Against Proposed "Mercy Killing" Legislation' (1958) 42 *Minnesota Law Review* 969.

J. Economics

VAE/PAS would save immense healthcare and social resources which will otherwise be spent on the dying, the demented and the elderly.

Not surprisingly this cold, utilitarian argument is seldom openly employed by advocates of VAE/PAS. It is, however, worth mentioning because it is the 'elephant in the room' of the debate, and an elephant which is only likely to grow with increasing pressure on healthcare and social resources. We will recall the former UK health minister's warning that PAS would come to be seen as cheaper than palliative care,[91] and Baroness Warnock's claim that the demented are 'wasting' NHS resources.[92] In the US, one state governor has reportedly claimed that 'We've got a duty to die', to free up resources for the young.[93] Derek Humphry – a pioneer of the modern euthanasia movement there – has written that 'in the final analysis, economics, not the quest for broadened individual liberties or increased autonomy, will drive assisted suicide to the plateau of acceptable practice'.[94] Economic pressures would likely play a far greater role in countries, such as the US, with less equitable access to healthcare. We will recall that patients in Oregon are already being bluntly told that although the state will not pay for therapy it will fund PAS, and that Patricia Mann has predicted that the relaxation of the law would change the social culture such that 'strong social expectations are likely to develop for individuals to choose assisted suicide as soon as their physical capacities decline to a point where they become extremely dependent upon others in an expensive, inconvenient way'.[95]

[91] See text at fn 26.

[92] See text at fn 15.

[93] See Editor's Note, www.nytimes.com/1984/03/29/us/gov-lamm-asserts-elderly-if-very-ill-have-duty-to-die.html. See also Gorsuch (n 44) 131. A nationwide US survey in May 2011 found that 35% of respondents thought that 'mentally able seniors' should be able to end their own lives to 'help save health care costs'. Kay Lazar, 'End-of-life economics' *The Boston Globe* (6 June 2011).

[94] D Humphry and M Clement, *Freedom to Die: People, Politics and the Right-to-Die Movement* (New York, St Martin's Press, 2000) 339.

[95] See text at fn 16.

Expensive their care will increasingly be. There is already a funding crisis affecting care of the elderly, which the charity Age UK has warned spells a 'more miserable existence for thousands of vulnerable and isolated older people across the country'.[96] Matters may well get much worse. A King's Fund report in 2010 on end-of-life care estimated that around 20 per cent of healthcare resources are already spent on end-of-life care, that the annual number of deaths is expected to rise by almost 20 per cent between 2012 and 2030, and that people will increasingly die at an older age, suffering from complex, multiple morbidities. An OECD report in 2011 predicted that low birth rates and rising life expectancy will require the UK to spend an extra £80 billion per year on pensions, long-term care and the health service by 2050. The report warned that the rising bill for elderly care could undermine the nexus of family relations between generations. The international cost of ageing populations has been estimated at 10 times that of the global financial crisis.[97] The vulnerable already find it difficult enough to access adequate medical and social care. Might they not see, and even be encouraged to see, VAE/PAS as an attractive alternative? Those unable to request an earlier demise would also be an obvious source of financial savings.

IV. PROFESSOR JACKSON'S ARGUMENTS

Section I canvassed 10 arguments standardly advanced in favour of legalising VAE/PAS. Let us now turn to the recent debate in the UK, to which Emily Jackson has made a significant contribution. Some of the arguments she has deployed differ from those we have already considered.

---

[96] D Martin, 'Elderly Care Costs Soar for Millions as Councils Feel Pinch' *The Daily Mail* (25 April 2011).

[97] T Ross, 'OECD: Huge Elderly Care Bill Threatens Family Ties' *The Daily Telegraph* (22 May 2011).

A. Jackson 1

In her first paper Professor Jackson replies to both principled and practical objections to decriminalisation.

i. *Principled Objections to Decriminalisation*

Jackson morally equates euthanasia with the withdrawal of life-prolonging treatment and with the administration of life-shortening palliative drugs. She asks why, despite permitting doctors' extensive involvement in 'ending their patients' lives' we continue to prohibit them from 'doing this' in the 'most humane and painless way', namely, by administering a single lethal injection. The answer is, as we noted above,[98] that withdrawing treatment on the ground that it is futile or too burdensome, and administering drugs in order to ease pain do not, unlike euthanasia, involve *intentionally* hastening the patient's death.

Her paper starts by claiming that withdrawal of life support is 'the most common cause of death in intensive care units'; that in palliative care 'it is routine to administer doses of analgesic drugs which are virtually certain to bring about the patient's death', and that if a patient asks to be disconnected from a ventilator the doctor must comply, even if the request appears 'wholly irrational'. All this seems to beg a number of questions. First, *is* the withdrawal of life support a 'cause' of death? Should it be entered as such on the patient's death certificate? Secondly, *is* it 'routine' to administer palliative drugs which shorten life? The evidence from the palliative care experts is that, properly titrated, opioids like morphine bring effective pain relief without shortening life. Thirdly, a 'wholly irrational' request to withdraw life-support may well raise questions about the patient's competency and, if the patient is incompetent, the doctor is not bound by the request.

Professor Jackson proceeds that the law's prohibition of euthanasia makes sense only if we ignore the perspective of the patient:

---

98 See pp 105–10, under 'Intention vs Foresight'.

'For the person whose life is at stake, a death which is brought about by treatment withdrawal will generally be indistinguishable from a death caused by a fatal injection'.[99] But patients surely distinguish between being relieved of a futile or excessively burdensome treatment and being injected with a lethal poison, and between being injected with diamorphine to ease pain and with potassium chloride to end life. She writes: 'From the patient's point of view, it does not matter whether the drug that induces death is diamorphine or potassium chloride.'[100] But if there is no difference to patients between a doctor who is trying to kill the patient's pain, and a doctor who is trying to kill the patient, what is the difference between the merciful ministrations of Dame Cicely Saunders and the murderous activities of Dr Harold Shipman? Is their respective conduct 'indistinguishable' to their patients (and to their patients' relatives)?

Jackson continues that the principle of patient autonomy is now 'dominant' and that the continuing prohibition on euthanasia reflects a 'peculiar and wilful disregard' of the patient's point of view, an 'extraordinary exception to the patient-centred development of medical law over the past fifty years'.[101] But is it not precisely a concern for the well-being of patients which explains the law's continuing prohibition on intentionally killing them? Nor does it follow that because the law recognises a patient's right to decide whether to undergo a proposed treatment and to be informed of the risks of and alternatives to that treatment, it should therefore confer a right to be killed. As we have seen,[102] there are many reasonable restrictions in modern medical law on what some patients may want: patients have no right to demand whatever treatments or drugs they want, and the law prohibits the selling of organs and FGM.

Professor Jackson considers, and rejects, a number of reasons for the law's prohibition of voluntary euthanasia. The first is the

[99] Jackson, 'Whose Death is it Anyway?' (n 1) 416.
[100] ibid 433.
[101] ibid 416.
[102] See pp 88–89, under 'Autonomy vs the Inviolability of Life'.

inviolability of life. She rejects the principle on the ground that 'we already allow competent adult patients to make this sort of judgment provided that they *happen* to need life-sustaining medical treatment'.[103] Doctors, she writes, are under a duty to remove life-prolonging treatment in such cases 'and thus are effectively under a duty to act deliberately to hasten the patient's death'.[104] This is so, she adds, even if the patient is likely to make a complete recovery and the patient's reasons for treatment withdrawal are bizarre, illogical or even non-existent. However, it does not follow, even assuming the patient's competence in such a scenario, and assuming that the doctor's conduct in stopping ventilation is accurately described as an 'act', that the doctor's *intention* is to end the patient's life. The doctor may simply take the view (consonant with traditional medical ethics) that the primary responsibility for looking after the patient's life and health is the patient's, not the doctor's. Even if the doctor thinks that the patient's refusal is competent and suicidal, as it may well have been in the case of *Re B* which Jackson invokes (the case, mentioned above,[105] of the competent patient with tetraplegia who was held to have a legal right to disconnection from the ventilation which was keeping her alive), it by no means follows that the doctor's *intention* in withdrawing treatment is to assist or encourage the patient's suicide. A decision to comply with a demand is not the same as an intention to assist a further purpose behind that demand, not least in a situation where (as with a competent refusal of medical treatment) the law requires compliance with that demand.

Professor Jackson next turns to the administration of palliative drugs. If we allow doctors to administer life-shortening doses of painkillers, she asks, why not allow them 'to accomplish exactly the same end' more swiftly?[106] The answer is that there is a major difference between trying to kill pain and trying to kill the patient. But even if palliative drugs did hasten death, it would not follow

---

[103] Jackson, 'Whose Death is it Anyway?' (n 1) 420.
[104] ibid.
[105] See p 113, under 'A Right to Suicide'.
[106] Jackson, 'Whose Death is it Anyway?' (n 1), 433.

that the doctors who administered them *intended* to hasten death. We will recall Seale's second survey showing that doctors who administered palliative drugs which may have shortened life only 'rarely' intended to shorten life. And, as we saw earlier, professional medical ethics and the law adopt the principle of 'double effect', which endorses the administration of drugs in order to ease pain, but not to kill. Jackson claims that in cases of double effect 'death is disingenuously described as an incidental *side-effect* of pain relief, when in reality death is the *means* to alleviate pain'.[107] But not every foreseen consequence is an intended consequence; not every effect is a means. The hastening of death from drugs administered to ease suffering is (if it occurs) no more a means to palliation than hair loss from chemotherapy is a means to curing cancer. Quoting Professor Glanville Williams (who also conflated intention and foresight), Professor Jackson claims that double effect encourages a doctor to 'keep his mind steadily off the consequence which his professional training teaches him is inevitable'.[108] Not so. The principle rules out *intending* a bad consequence, not *foreseeing* it. She also claims that double effect is not concerned with the patient's point of view:

> Without any necessity to investigate whether the patient shared her doctor's belief that relieving pain is more important than prolonging life, the doctrine of double effect permits doctors to make much more paternalistic quality of life judgments than would be possible if voluntary euthanasia were to be legalised.[109]

Again, not so. Double effect guides doctors as to when it is permissible to carry out a treatment which may or will have an unintended bad side-effect. It does not absolve doctors from obtaining the patient's consent to that treatment or from informing the patient about its effects. Nor does it allow doctors to make the objectionable 'quality of life' judgment that a patient, whether competent or not, would be 'better off dead'. It is *euthanasia* which

---

[107]   ibid 440.
[108]   ibid 435.
[109]   ibid 440.

involves making such a judgment. Jackson acknowledges as much when she writes that a doctor may reasonably judge that death would benefit the patient:

> Unlike competent treatment refusals which are governed only by the principle of patient autonomy, in relation to legalised euthanasia the principles of beneficence and non-maleficence would trump patient autonomy. The doctor would only be acting properly if she had considered not only the patient's wish to die, but also her own ethical responsibility for the promotion of well-being, and her duty to do no harm. Unless the doctor genuinely *and reasonably* believed that death would benefit the patient by relieving her unbearable distress, there could be no justification for deliberately causing her death.[110]

Having sought to squeeze respect for treatment refusals and the administration of palliative drugs into the same moral category as the intentional hastening of death, Professor Jackson seeks to do the same with the withdrawal of life-prolonging treatment from incompetent patients. Discussing *Bland,* she writes that a decision to continue the 'treatment' of a patient in PVS 'cannot be made without imposing *our* judgment about whether a permanently insensate life is worth living'.[111] This is unconvincing. First, a decision to withhold/withdraw treatment from an incompetent patient, including one in PVS, need involve no judgment about whether the patient's life is 'worth living'. Treatments are withheld/withdrawn from patients (competent and incompetent) every day of the week without any such judgment. In *Bland* itself, for example, Lord Goff reasoned that the patient's tube-feeding could be withdrawn because, like a ventilator would have been, it was futile and could do nothing to improve his condition. This reasoning is quite different from judging that the patient's life was no longer 'worth living'. Secondly, the fact that a majority of the Law Lords in *Bland* thought it lawful to withdraw tube-feeding even with intent to kill is not a refutation of the

---

[110] ibid 439.
[111] ibid 423.

inviolability of life but a failure to apply it. The law has often failed to track sound ethics and, to be fair to the distinguished judges in *Bland*, they were not helped by inaccurate submissions about the inviolability of life made by learned counsel in that case, including counsel representing Tony Bland's interests. Jackson is right to observe that this case left the law in a morally contradictory state, permitting the intentional starvation of the incompetent but prohibiting lethal injections for those who want them. But this is no more an argument for remedying the inconsistency by permitting the latter than it is for prohibiting the former. As we have noted,[112] Parliament has acted to prohibit the former by enacting s 4(5) of the Mental Capacity Act 2005.

Professor Jackson's final criticism of the inviolability of life involves pointing out that courts do not condemn doctors who, because of financial constraints, withhold potentially life-saving treatment from patients who want it. However, doctors are under no duty, ethical or legal, to do what they do not have the resources to do. The government, health service managers and doctors must make decisions about how resources can best be allocated. To fund treatment for condition A instead of condition B need involve no judgment that those with condition B have lives which are worth less than those with condition A, much less that those with condition B have lives which are no longer worth living. It may simply be that the treatment for condition B is more costly and/or less effective than the treatment for condition A.

The recurrent problem with Professor Jackson's argument is its conflation of intention and foresight. This produces a confusion between, on the one hand, euthanasia and, on the other, medical conduct which need involve no intention to end life. If her argument were right, there would be no euthanasia debate at all. As even the Dutch agree, euthanasia is about the intentional, not merely foreseen, ending of life. Emily Jackson's own textbook on medical law uses 'euthanasia' to 'refer only to voluntary active

---

[112] See text at fn 35.

euthanasia, that is where a doctor deliberately acts to kill a patient at her request'.[113]

ii. Practical Objections to Decriminalisation

In the second part of her article, Professor Jackson seeks to refute the arguments that if euthanasia were legalised it would be difficult to ensure that requests were voluntary, and that it would lead to a 'slippery slope'. First: voluntariness. She agrees that it would be of 'vital importance to ensure that patients' requests for euthanasia had been made voluntarily',[114] and claims that the 'obvious response' to concerns about voluntariness is that:

> we already allow patients to make decisions which will result in their deaths when we respect their refusals of life-prolonging medical treatment. A patient who is connected to a mechanical ventilator may be depressed, and we may wrongly judge her to be competent, but this inescapable risk of error does not persuade us that we should prevent patients from taking life or death decisions.[115]

The analogy is problematic. There is a consensus that patients have the right to refuse treatment. The rule, established in professional medical ethics and the law, is that a doctor is not entitled to treat a competent patient without consent. And rightly so: the alternative of potentially requiring all patients to undergo life-prolonging treatments would be 'vitalism' and morally indefensible. But there is no consensus that patients have a right to euthanasia. Indeed, the rule, established in professional medical ethics and the law, is that doctors must not intentionally kill their patients. The risk of treatment refusals being incompetent or pressured is indeed an 'inescapable risk' which we should minimise as best we can. By contrast, the risk of euthanasia requests being incompetent or pressured is *not* 'inescapable': it is not a risk we have to take. The alternative of prohibiting euthanasia is per-

---

[113] E Jackson, *Medical Law: Text, Cases and Materials* (Oxford, Oxford University Press, 2006) 911.

[114] Jackson, 'Whose Death is it Anyway?' (n 1) 427.

[115] ibid 428.

fectly reasonable and has long been the legal norm worldwide. Secondly, a treatment refusal may not shorten life at all: euthanasia does. Jackson herself notes that in relation to euthanasia there is no scope for correcting the mistake that patient was not competent or did not have a terminal disease. Thirdly, even if the treatment would have prolonged life, it may have been a treatment the doctor would have withdrawn as futile or too costly regardless of whether the patient's refusal was competent. Fourthly, doctors are better placed to detect an incompetent or pressured refusal of treatment than an incompetent or pressured request for euthanasia. The largely objective and clinical question whether a *treatment* is beneficial to a patient is within the expertise of a doctor, and the refusal of a beneficial treatment is therefore more likely to alert the doctor to questions of competence and voluntariness, unlike the largely subjective and moral question (which traditional professional ethics eschews) whether the patient's *life* is beneficial.

Moreover, given Professor Jackson's proper concern about the 'vital importance' of ensuring that requests for euthanasia are competent and not pressured, it hardly assists her argument to highlight the *existing* risk that requests to discontinue treatment may be incompetent or pressured. Her argument seems to be: because we already take some risks of (unintentionally) hastening the deaths of patients who are incompetent or who are pressured into refusing treatment, we should take even more risks by allowing the (intentional) hastening of deaths of many others who are not receiving life-prolonging treatment. By analogy, should we repeal the law prohibiting FGM because, although there are risks that women will be pressured to have their genitals mutilated, we already accept the risk that they may be pressured to undergo other procedures, such as abortion? Allowing euthanasia would clearly increase the risk of patients making requests which were incompetent or the result of pressure. It would provide yet another avenue for grasping or uncaring or exhausted relatives to bring pressure to bear on those 'inconsiderate' enough to want to go on living, especially those who are, inconveniently, not being sustained by life-prolonging treatment which they might be pressured to stop.

Jackson continues that in so far as a risk of abuse exists, a 'carefully regulated system might in fact offer much more effective protection than the blunt instrument of a blanket ban which in practice simply pushes the practice underground'.[116] But she does not show that there is a significant underground practice in the UK or US; that legalisation would not substantially increase such practice as exists, or that a 'carefully regulated system' (whatever that would look like) is feasible. She draws an analogy with the Abortion Act 1967 and points out that some advocates of decriminalisation argued that it would replace abortion in insanitary conditions with a system of safeguards and control that would promote safe abortions. This analogy is also problematic. As we saw above,[117] abortions notified by doctors have dramatically increased since that Act, and it is widely accepted that the Act's so-called 'safeguards' have failed to prevent abortion being widely available on request, not least on social grounds, grounds which are outwith the Act. Even Lord Steel, who as David Steel MP steered the legislation through Parliament, observed almost 30 years ago that abortion was being used 'as a contraceptive'.[118] Moreover, the Act does little to ensure that women are not pressured into abortion. A woman's request for abortion requires the approval of two registered medical practitioners but neither need have any expertise in psychiatry; the first doctor may carry out only the most cursory interview with the woman, and the second doctor may not even see her. One can only imagine the lasting psychological effects of being pressured into an abortion. But at least the woman remains alive, unlike a woman pressured into euthanasia. (Concerns have, relevantly, been raised about particular risks to women from decriminalising euthanasia.[119]) Lord Habgood has observed that, regardless of what one

---

[116] ibid 429.

[117] See p 116–17, under 'Legal Failure'.

[118] P Bartram, *David Steel: His Life and Politics* (London, Star, 1982) 85.

[119] K George, 'A Woman's Choice? The Gendered Risks of Voluntary Euthanasia and Physician-Assisted Suicide' (2007) 15 *Medical Law Review* 1.

thinks of abortion, it has since decriminalisation become a live option for *anyone* who is pregnant, and that the climate of opinion in which an unwanted pregnancy is now faced has radically altered. Decriminalising euthanasia would, he predicts, be no less culture-changing. It would bring about 'profound changes in social attitudes towards death, illness, old age and the role of the medical profession'.[120]

Let us now turn to Professor Jackson's discussion of the 'slippery slope'. Her statement of the 'slippery slope' argument is that even if it were reasonable for doctors to comply with patients' requests for euthanasia in some cases, we should nevertheless prohibit euthanasia because it would be 'very difficult to prevent those with less benevolent motives' from ending patients' lives.[121] This statement of the argument is incomplete. First, one may deploy the argument even if one does not think it *ever* reasonable to kill patients. Secondly, the slide may not only be from benevolent to less benevolent motives, but also from a free to a forced request, from unbearable to bearable suffering, and from terminal to chronic physical or mental illness and even to non-medical conditions like 'tiredness of life'. Thirdly, as we saw earlier, there is not only an empirical 'slippery slope' argument, but also a no less formidable logical argument.

Professor Jackson's answer to the empirical argument that she addresses is unconvincing. She writes that 'this "grey area" problem exists whenever we attempt to regulate *anything*'.[122] She invokes a 'more mundane' regulatory problem, namely, the question whether she should impose an absolute prohibition on the submission of late essays by students. She argues that allowing an extension for a very compelling reason, such as student A's bereavement, might make it more difficult for her to exclude less persuasive grounds, such as student C's computer malfunction, but that an absolute ban does 'a grave injustice' to student A. However, it is not obvious that an absolute deadline does student A any injustice,

---

[120] Keown (n 17) 275.
[121] Jackson, 'Whose Death is it Anyway?' (n 1) 430.
[122] ibid.

let alone a grave injustice. There are many situations in life where we may face absolute deadlines, such as casting a vote, checking in for a flight, or (to maintain the student analogy) getting to an examination hall on time. The fact that we may have a good reason for not arriving on time does not mean we are treated unjustly if we are not allowed to vote, board the plane, or sit the exam. Moreover, Jackson's analogy is, as she describes it, 'mundane'. Killing patients is anything but. Whether a university teacher has a policy of allowing late essay submissions is hardly a matter of life and death. If she allows late submissions the worst that can happen is that some students will get their essays marked on the back of an unmeritorious excuse. If we allow euthanasia, the worst than can happen is that patients will be killed without their consent and even against their will. There is obviously a world of difference between marking and murder. A more apt analogy would have been between VAE and capital punishment. Many people oppose capital punishment not because they think that executing a murderer like Myra Hindley or Charles Manson is wrong, but because of the danger of executing an innocent person. Whatever safeguards are proposed, they argue, the risk, however small, of convicting the innocent is such that capital punishment should not be allowed. It is better that 10 serial killers be spared execution than that one innocent person be hanged. The argument is not unreasonable. Yet when one considers the battery of safeguards against wrongful conviction, including the right to counsel and to a fair trial, in which the prosecution must prove guilt beyond all reasonable doubt, the so-called 'safeguards' typically proposed against wrongful euthanasia pale into insignificance.

Professor Jackson then turns to the contention that the Dutch experience lends weighty support to the 'slippery slope' argument. She claims that this is only true 'if there is a *causal link* between the legalisation of euthanasia in the Netherlands and the Dutch medical profession's (alleged) willingness to end patients' lives without prior request'.[123] First, the word 'alleged' is puzzling.

---

[123]   ibid 431.

As we have seen, the Dutch admit that doctors have euthanised thousands of patients without request and that NVAE is officially condoned in certain circumstances. Secondly, it is not necessary to prove a causal link to establish, as Jackson herself expresses, the 'slippery slope' argument, that it is 'very difficult to locate or police the line between acceptable and unacceptable practices'.[124] The Dutch claimed, when they originally relaxed their legal prohibition on VAE/PAS, that to kill a patient without request would remain murder and would be prosecuted as such. Opponents of relaxation warned that the Dutch authorities would not be able to police that line. The data generated by the Dutch themselves confirm that they have, indeed, failed to do so. The burden is not on opponents to prove a causal link between legalisation and abuse: the burden is on advocates of legalisation to substantiate their claim that VAE/PAS can be safely policed. This they have signally failed to do. Jackson suggests that the evidence from the Netherlands is 'equivocal'. But what is 'equivocal' about the thousands of cases of NVAE (and hundreds of IVAE), the thousands of unreported cases, and the slide to the official endorsement of NVAE?

Because advocates of VAE/PAS struggle to show that they can be effectively policed, they tend to divert attention to the alleged failings of the law in countries which ban them. Professor Jackson invokes a postal survey of doctors in Australia, carried out by Professor Peter Singer and Dr Helga Kuhse, which (allegedly) shows that passive euthanasia without request is more common there than in the Netherlands. However, questions about the reliability of this survey, which was carried out by two of the world's leading advocates of euthanasia, have been raised by several experts, including Professor Seale. And Seale has concluded that because the rate of killing without consent is so low in the UK, the argument that criminalisation breeds fear of bringing the issues out into the open 'cannot be made'.[125]

---

[124] ibid 430.
[125] Seale (n 41) 6–8.

Jackson concludes that a blanket ban is a blunt approach, especially as the consequence for patients who she thinks merit euthanasia 'will be a protracted, painful, or otherwise intolerable death'.[126] She claims that patients like Dianne Pretty have 'no option but to endure an unendurable death'.[127] Yet the head of medical services at the hospice where Dianne Pretty died described her death as 'perfectly normal, natural and peaceful'.[128] Jackson writes that without 'more persuasive evidence, hypothetical speculation about an as yet unwritten law's possible future inefficacy' does not justify a failure to think about how we might effectively regulate euthanasia. However, in view of the disturbing evidence from the Netherlands in particular, evidence which has clearly weighed with bodies such as the Walton Committee and the New York State Task Force, we are surely well beyond the realm of 'hypothetical speculation'. Professor Jackson claims that most of us would like to die quickly and at home in the presence of someone we love, and that the present law does not promote such a death. As the present law does not prohibit dying at home or in the presence of someone we love, her claim can only relate to dying 'quickly', which presumably means having VAE/PAS. But where is the evidence that this is what most of us want? As for having 'loved ones' around the bed, do we really want to move to a world where death is choreographed to suit relatives' availability? And let us not forget the many who are unloved and whose relatives will not be at the bedside, but only at the reading of the will. Jackson asks us to imagine a competent patient with motor neurone disease who wants, and whose doctor is willing to administer, a lethal injection. She asserts that the current law 'insists that the patient must die a protracted and potentially extremely distressing death'.[129] But if the patient dies quickly and painlessly, what law has been broken? She argues that what patients fear is not doctors shortening life precipitately, but prolonging it exces-

---

[126] Jackson, 'Whose Death is it Anyway?' (n 1) 432.
[127] ibid 441.
[128] 'Diane Pretty dies' *BBC News* (12 May 2002).
[129] Jackson, 'Whose Death is it Anyway?' (n 1) 436.

sively; they fear doctors 'doing everything humanly possible to postpone death'.[130] This is hardly an argument for euthanasia and for undermining traditional medical ethics: it is an argument for doctors respecting traditional medical ethics and not imposing treatments which are futile or unduly burdensome on the patient. Jackson continues that what is important about the medical profession's ethical prohibition on euthanasia is that it allows no exceptions: 'no other rules of ethical conduct have this absolute quality'.[131] Not so. To take one of several possible examples, there is no exception to the ethical (and legal) prohibition of FGM. It cannot be right, Professor Jackson proceeds, given that some people are 'so terrified by the prospect of a protracted, undignified, and perhaps painful death' and would prefer a lethal injection, that we 'insist that such patients should have to endure precisely the sort of death that they fear in order to protect *other* as yet hypothetical people from being pressurised into requesting euthanasia'.[132] A blanket ban, she adds, could be justified only if it were 'impossible' to distinguish those who want VAE from those who may have been pressured to request it. However, many people's fears about how they are likely to die are groundless. The belief, for example, that motor neurone disease means death by choking is mistaken. Moreover, the present law permits, indeed requires, doctors to use all reasonable means to alleviate the pain and distress of the dying: it does not 'insist' that patients 'endure precisely the sort of death that they fear'. Further, those protected by the current law are not 'hypothetical'. They are (like the poor victims of Dr Shipman) every bit as real as those who might want VAE/PAS, and far more numerous too. The law is there to affirm the dignity, and ensure the protection, of everyone, both the few who may want VAE/PAS and the many who do not and upon whom it might be pressed. Nor do supporters of the present law need to prove it would be 'impossible' to distinguish between the two groups, any more than opponents of capital

---

[130] ibid 437.
[131] ibid.
[132] ibid 438.

punishment need to show it is 'impossible' to distinguish between those guilty and not guilty of capital crimes. Why does a grave risk, or even a substantial risk, of getting it wrong not justify a blanket ban? Why isn't the burden on *advocates* of VAE/PAS to show that it would be 'impossible' if the law were relaxed for patients to be killed against their will? Which is worse: under the present law dying a natural death (assisted by modern palliative care) when one would have preferred an earlier death? Or, under a law allowing VAE/PAS, being murdered? The proper question is not why protection of the many should trump the wishes of the few but why the wishes of the few should trump the protection of the many. By analogy, should the blanket ban on FGM be relaxed in cases where a woman freely wants to have her clitoris excised? Is the protection of 'other as yet hypothetical women' who might be pressured if the ban were lifted an insufficient justification? Professor Jackson argues that the 'safeguards' for euthanasia, to ensure that the patient's request were voluntary and that death would be a benefit, would be stricter than in relation to treatment refusal, palliative treatment, or the withdrawal of treatment from the incompetent.[133] But by again overlooking the facts that euthanasia involves intentional killing and creates risks we simply do not need to take, this analogy again fails.

In the *Pretty* case, Dianne Pretty asked the courts to order the Director of Public Prosecutions (DPP) to guarantee that he would not prosecute her husband if he assisted her to commit suicide. She argued (an argument repeated by Professor Jackson) that whatever the need might be for legal protection of the vulnerable, she was not vulnerable, and that there was therefore no justification for the law's blanket prohibition. The Senior Law Lord, Lord Bingham, responded:

> Beguiling as that submission is, Dr Johnson gave two answers of enduring validity to it. First, 'Laws are not made for particular cases but for men in general.' Second, 'To permit a law to be modified at discretion is to leave the community without law.' It is to withdraw

---

[133] Jackson, 'Whose Death is it Anyway?' (n 1) 439–40.

the direction of that public wisdom by which the deficiencies of private understanding are to be supplied.[134]

To Pretty's argument that the law unjustly discriminated against those who, like her, were physically unable to commit suicide without assistance, Lord Bingham responded that the criminal law could not be criticised as discriminatory because it applied to everyone:

> Although in some instances criminal statutes recognise exceptions based on youth, the broad policy of the criminal law is to apply offence-creating provisions to all and to give weight to personal circumstances either at the stage of considering whether or not to prosecute or, in the event of conviction, when penalty is to be considered. The criminal law does not ordinarily distinguish between willing victims and others . . . Provisions criminalising drunkenness or misuse of drugs or theft do not exempt those addicted to alcohol or drugs, or the poor and hungry.

He added:

> 'Mercy killing', as it is often called, is in law killing. If the criminal law sought to proscribe the conduct of those who assisted the suicide of the vulnerable, but exonerated those who assisted the suicide of the non-vulnerable, it could not be administered fairly and in a way which would command respect.[135]

Citing sources including the Walton Report, his Lordship concluded that there were 'ample grounds to justify the existing law and the application of it'.[136] Lord Steyn observed that the law's total prohibition on assisting suicide was 'a legitimate, rational and proportionate response to the wider problem of vulnerable people who would otherwise feel compelled to commit suicide'.[137] On appeal, the European Court of Human Rights agreed that a blanket ban did not breach the European Convention on Human Rights:

[134] *Pretty* (n 37) [29].
[135] At [36].
[136] At [30].
[137] At [63].

Doubtless the condition of terminally ill individuals will vary. But many will be vulnerable and it is the vulnerability of the class which provides the rationale for the law in question . . . Clear risks of abuse do exist, notwithstanding arguments as to the possibility of safeguards.[138]

More recently, the Court has held that states are under no obligation to facilitate assisted suicide. Upholding a Swiss law which allows lethal drugs to be supplied only on prescription, the Court observed that the risks of abuse if a state permitted assisted suicide could not be underestimated.[139]

Regrettably, the European Court indicated in *Pretty* that the UK's blanket ban *did* engage Dianne Pretty's right to respect for 'private and family life' guaranteed by Article 8(1) of the Convention, though the ban was saved by Article 8(2) which allows interference with that right if the interference is in accordance with law and necessary in a democratic society in the protection of certain interests, including the rights and freedoms of others. The Court's interpretation of Article 8(1) was surely unsound. How can assisting suicide, a matter of the gravest *public* concern, ever be a *private* matter? The Court would have done better to follow Lord Bingham, who held that Article 8(1) sought to protect certain choices while people were living their lives, not the choice to live no longer. No less regrettably, the Law Lords have now gone even further than the European Court in misinterpreting Article 8(1). In the *Purdy* case they went so far as to order the DPP to issue guidance spelling out the factors he would take into account in deciding whether to prosecute Debbie Purdy's husband should he assist her to commit suicide. Their decision, reversing a strong Court of Appeal, was unsound if not unconstitutional. As the Lord Chief Justice had observed in the

---

[138] *Pretty v United Kingdom* (2002) 35 EHRR 1 [74].

[139] 'En particulier, la Cour considère que l'on ne saurait sous-estimer les risques d'abus inhérents à un système facilitant l'accès au suicide assisté': *Affaire Haas c Suisse* (2011) [58], http://cmiskp.echr.coe.int/tkp197/view.asp?action=html&documentId=880260&portal=hbkm&source=externalbydocnumber&table=F69A27FD8FB86142BF01C1166DEA398649.

Court of Appeal, making such an order 'would, in effect, recognise exceptional defences to this offence which Parliament has not chosen to enact.'[140] Indeed, Parliament has *chosen not* to enact such exceptions. The Law Lords, by making the order, undermined Parliament's ban on assisting suicide. So too have the guidelines subsequently issued by the DPP, which send the clear signal that if they are followed, no prosecution will ensue.[141]

Now let us turn to the logical slippery slope argument. Professor Jackson mentions the argument only in passing, claiming that slippery slope arguments are essentially empirical. No matter: her article serves only to confirm the logical argument. She states that for reasons of space the focus of her article is on competent adults but adds: 'Plainly, however, the humanitarian justification for allowing doctors to help their patients to die must apply equally to incompetent patients.'[142] She is, of course, correct. Her second article expands on and explains her endorsement of NVAE.

B. Jackson 2

Echoing the argument we considered earlier,[143] Professor Jackson's second article, 'Secularism, Sanctity and the Wrongness of Killing', criticises as 'religious' the belief that human life has intrinsic value. It also contends[144] that human life has only instrumental, not intrinsic, value, and that it is ethical for doctors to euthanise patients for whom death would not be a 'harm'.

Citing Ronald Dworkin, the article claims that the sanctity of life, with its commitment to the intrinsic value of human lives, makes no sense 'other than as an article of religious faith'.[145] It

---

[140] *R (on the application of Purdy) v Director of Public Prosecutions* [2009] EWCA Civ 92 [79]. See J Keown, 'In Need of Assistance?' (2009) 159 *New Law Journal* 1340.

[141] For a critique of the interim guidance see J Keown, 'Dangerous Guidance' (2009) 159 *New Law Journal* 1718.

[142] Jackson, 'Whose Death is it Anyway?' (n 1) 417.

[143] See pp 136–37, under 'Religion'.

[144] Echoing arguments mentioned under 'Legal Hypocrisy', pp 105–10.

[145] Jackson, 'Secularism, Sanctity and the Wrongness of Killing' (n 1) 126.

argues that most of the candidates for distinctively human quali-
ties which make our lives more valuable than animals, such as
consciousness, moral reasoning and self-awareness, are characteristics which are possessed by most but not all humans, such as
those in PVS and anencephalic babies. Following Peter Singer, it
contends that to value a patient in PVS higher than a chimpanzee
is mere 'speciesism'. It claims that some animals are self-aware
and capable of engaging in complex reasoning and planning for
the future and it asks where the supposed 'inherent dignity' of all
members of the human family, asserted in the Preamble to the
Universal Declaration of Human Rights, comes from. The article
submits that there are 'no rational grounds' for believing that
there is an important difference between all humans and all animals, and that a belief in the unique value of humans can only be
a matter of faith. Attaching value not to human beings but to
'persons', it cites differing criteria for 'personhood' which proponents of this approach have advanced, such as Jeff McMahan's
requirement of a capacity for self-consciousness, of a 'rich
and complex mental life, a mental life of a high order of
sophistication'.[146] On such an approach, it points out, Tony Bland
died as a 'person' when he fell into PVS, and died as an 'organism'
after his tube-feeding and hydration were withdrawn some years
later. The article then turns to the implications of this approach
for the ethics of killing.

Killing is wrong, it contends, when it 'harms' a person. Killing
is normally a great wrong because it is normally a very great harm:
'Killing is wrong instrumentally because it destroys everything
that has been invested in the person's life, as well as depriving the
person who is killed of all future experiences'.[147] However, 'where
we can be certain that a human being's future contains no experiences at all, or only pain and suffering which has become unbearable, death may no longer be an instrumental harm'.[148] It quotes
Dan Brock's view that the right to life should be 'waivable' when

---

[146]   ibid 137.
[147]   ibid 138.
[148]   ibid 139.

'the person makes a competent decision that continued life is no longer wanted or a good, but is instead worse than no further life at all'.[149] Professor Jackson is 'not sure' that she would go so far, for a doctor who gave a lethal injection to a 'lovesick teenager' would be 'ignoring the fundamental duties of a doctor'.[150] In the 'vast majority of cases', she reasons, death would be a harm because for most people life will contain both good as well as bad experiences and because we would be speculating about the future, making it impossible confidently to conclude that it would be better for someone to die now. She continues that Tony Bland's death was not a harm and notes that some of the judges thought he had an interest in an end being put to 'the humiliation of his being and the distress of his family'.[151] Her paper concludes that it will 'occasionally be possible' to say that the 'balance sheet' militates in favour of an earlier death and that the views of the person whose life it is as to whether their life is worth living is evidence of an 'overwhelmingly powerful kind'.[152]

The paper rejects the danger of a 'slippery slope', of death being forced upon vulnerable and dependent individuals, because 'it is only possible to conclude that death is a good thing for a person if we can be certain that it would be better for them if they died now, and that this would be consistent with their wishes and values'.[153] If, it adds, we can confidently conclude that death now as opposed to later is preferable for a patient 'either by applying the best interests test for an incompetent patient, or by respecting the competent patient's own choice about whether their life is worth living', where it can be achieved by treatment withdrawal, it seems odd that we cannot make the same assessment when a positive act is necessary to achieve death.[154]

The line of argument developed in this second paper is unpersuasive. First, the many atheists and agnostics who subscribe to

---

[149] ibid.
[150] ibid 140.
[151] ibid 141.
[152] ibid 142–43.
[153] ibid 143.
[154] ibid.

the concept of inherent human dignity which underpins the Universal Declaration of Human Rights will be surprised to discover that they are religious believers after all, and will doubtless be intrigued to discover to which religion they are thought to belong. And for the paper to invoke Ronald Dworkin as a defender of the sanctity of life, when he has long been one of its most outspoken critics, is akin to invoking Margaret Thatcher as a defender of communism. Dworkin simply steals the inviolability of life's clothes in his attempt to subvert it.

Secondly, as we saw in section III,[155] the view that human life has an intrinsic value can be amply supported on solely philosophical grounds. In his recent book *The Ethics of Abortion* Christopher Kaczor crisply refutes the arguments about the value of life and 'personhood' relied on by Professor Jackson. Her paper misapprehends a cardinal reason for the intrinsic value of human life: our radical capacity for rationality, conceptual thought and free will. That we have this valuable capacity does not entail that we are always able to exercise it. We may be asleep, or a baby, or in a coma, or senile. A radical *capacity* must not be confused with a presently exercisable *ability*. A baby has the natural capacity to reason, even though he or she is not yet able to exercise it. I have the capacity to speak German, though I am not able to do so. A person with dementia has the capacity to reason, even though damage to their brain prevents them from exercising it. Because we are all, by our very nature, beings with this radical capacity, we are intrinsically, and not merely instrumentally, valuable. This basis for rights, including the right not to be intentionally killed, is no more 'speciesist' than it is 'religious'. It would extend to any creature, earthly or alien, which possessed the same capacity for rationality, conceptual thought and free will.

Thirdly, having misapprehended the inviolability of life as 'religious' and 'speciesist', the paper proposes an alternative which is as vague as it is arbitrary. Its discrimination between human beings who are 'persons' and 'non-persons' is an illustration of the slip-

---

[155] See pp 87–91, under 'Autonomy vs the Inviolability of Life'.

pery slope which awaits anyone who abandons the firm philosophical platform provided by rights grounded in our common
humanity. It is far from clear how 'non-persons' are to be identified. This is problematic, given the potentially lethal consequences
of being so categorised. The paper gestures at various criteria
which have been proposed by philosophers but is hazy about
which it thinks decisive, and to which degree. Is it, perhaps,
McMahan's 'rich and complex mental life, a mental life of a high
order of sophistication'? But what does that mean? How 'rich' is
'rich', how 'high' is 'high'? Any such approach is, clearly, inherently
arbitrary and provides no sound basis for deciding whom we have
a duty to treat justly and whom the law should protect. The disturbing implications for babies, the senile, the comatose, those
with learning disabilities and perhaps even those with a low IQ are
clear. Professor Jackson rightly criticises the Nazis for drawing 'a
morally repugnant line between lives that were of value and lives
that were not, based upon membership of racial, religious and
other social groups'.[156] But does not her paper propose the same
kind of line, albeit in relation to differently defined social groups?
And might not some of the groups, perhaps those with severe
learning disabilities, turn out to be the same as those targeted by
the Nazis? In his classic commentary on the ghastly practices of
the Nazi doctors, Dr Leo Alexander, a consultant during the
Nuremberg trials, noted: 'In Germany, the exterminations included
the mentally defective, psychotics (particularly schizophrenics),
epileptics and patients suffering from infirmities of old age and
from various organic neurologic disorders such as infantile paraly-
sis, Parkinsonism, multiple sclerosis and brain tumors'. And it all
started, he added, 'with the acceptance of the attitude, basic in the
euthanasia movement, that there is such a thing as a life not worthy to be lived'.[157] Once one has accepted that certain human
beings are 'non-persons' or mere 'organisms', they clearly become
prime candidates for exploitation and elimination. Professor

---

[156] Jackson, 'Secularism, Sanctity and the Wrongness of Killing' (n 1) 136.
[157] L Alexander, 'Medical Science under Dictatorship' (1949) 241 *New England Journal of Medicine* 39, 44. Emphasis added.

Jackson writes that an important difference between a severely impaired human being and 'a non-human animal' is that the human being has relatives and that the relatives might be harmed if someone they loved was, say, treated as a resource for scientific experiments. But this is cold comfort. What if the 'severely impaired human being' has no relatives, or has uncaring relatives, or has relatives who would *like* them to be used for research or for spare parts? With typical candour, Emily Jackson accepts that where there are no family or friends, there is no one likely to be harmed if we were 'to treat her in the same way as an animal'.[158] Her paper invites us to step into a world where the most vulnerable members of the human family are not the beneficiaries of human solidarity, but the victims of blatant exploitation. No one who subscribes to an adequate conception of basic human rights could dream of entertaining such an invitation.

What of those human beings who manage to clear the bar of 'personhood', whichever criterion is selected and however high it is set? We will recall that Jackson concludes that it will 'occasionally' be possible to say with certainty that the 'balance sheet' militates in favour of an earlier death, and that the views of the person whose life it is as to whether their life is 'worth living' are evidence of an 'overwhelmingly powerful kind'.[159] But if the views of the person are 'overwhelmingly powerful' evidence, why will death only 'occasionally' be better than life? What, for example, of the many thousands of elderly people who might want to die because they are physically suffering, or are 'tired of life', or feel a burden, or are lonely, neglected or abused? If they think that their lives are no longer worth living, why should their autonomous request for euthanasia not be respected? Would refusal not be a 'peculiar and wilful disregard' of the patient's point of view?[160] We will recall Professor Jackson's comment that if we can confidently conclude that death now as opposed to later is prefer-

---

[158] Jackson, 'Secularism, Sanctity and the Wrongness of Killing' (n 1) 134.
[159] See text at fn 152.
[160] See text at fn 101.

able for a patient 'by respecting the competent patient's own choice about whether their life is worth living' where it can be achieved by treatment withdrawal, it seems odd that we cannot make the same assessment when a positive act is necessary to achieve death.[161] What of the 'lovesick teenager'? Professor Jackson thinks that a doctor who gives a lethal injection to a love-sick teenager would be 'ignoring the fundamental duties of a doctor'.[162] But if the teenager's request is autonomous, is it not a fundamental duty of the doctor to respect it just as if the teen-ager had requested disconnection from a ventilator? Another 'right to die' advocate, Dr Philip Nitschke, has no such reserva-tions. He thinks that people have a right to dispose of their life whenever they want and that it is ethical to help anyone exercise that right, including 'the depressed, the elderly bereaved, [and] the troubled teen'.[163] Even Professor Jackson, we recall, is 'not sure' that she rejects an entirely subjective approach. Further, why do we need to be 'certain' that someone would be better off dead? (Do we need to be 'certain' that withdrawal of life-support would benefit the patient?) What if we are 'certain' that a person's 'balance sheet' favours death but the person, inconsiderately, disagrees? Why should we not try to persuade them of their error, especially if their refusal will soak up valuable healthcare or social resources? If they do not listen to reason, why should we not withdraw those resources or even end their lives? If they are on a ventilator and death would benefit them, what would be wrong with disconnecting the ventilator, even against their will, espe-cially if we could put the machine to better use? As Professor Jackson would presumably see no moral difference between with-drawing ventilation against their will, and giving them an injection against their will, why not give the injection, at least if, inconven-iently, the withdrawal of ventilation does not kill them? We saw

---

[161] See text at fn154.
[162] See text at fn150.
[163] KJ Lopez, 'Euthanasia Sets Sail. An Interview with Philip Nitschke' (5 June 2001) http://old.nationalreview.com/interrogatory/interrogatory060501.shtml.

earlier that she accepts that autonomy can be trumped by beneficence. Why not here?

Professor Jackson, unlike some advocates of the 'right to die', is commendably frank about the two main pillars on which her conclusions rest: the moral equation of intending and foreseeing death, and the belief that the lives of some human beings lack worth. Those pillars would justify both VAE and NVAE in a very wide range of cases. And, although she explicitly opposes IVAE, it is not difficult to see how they could be invoked to justify it too, at least in certain cases. The last major push to relax the law in England did not go so far. It was Lord Joffe's attempt to decriminalise PAS for the terminally ill. Supporters of the Bill claimed that its 'safeguards' would prevent any abuse and any slide down the slippery slope. Let us now consider the cogency of those claims.

V. THE JOFFE BILL

Friday 12 May 2006 witnessed the second reading debate in the House of Lords on Lord Joffe's Assisted Dying for the Terminally Ill Bill. The Bill was an amended version of a previous Bill which had been scrutinised the year before by the Mackay Committee. As we shall see, the Bill failed to incorporate several key recommendations made by the Committee. We shall also see that the Bill invited both extension and abuse: the principles advanced to justify PAS would also have justified both VAE and NVAE, and the 'safeguards' in the Bill were weak. We shall conclude with a hypothetical example illustrating their limitations.[164]

A. The Bill

The Bill sought to 'enable an adult who has capacity and who is suffering unbearably as a result of a terminal illness to receive

---

[164] See generally Keown (n 56).

medical assistance to die at his own considered and persistent request'. Broadly, the Bill was modelled on Oregon's DWDA, though it seemed to allow some room for VAE and it incorporated a Dutch-style monitoring system.

B. Key Committee Recommendations Not Adopted

The Mackay Committee had identified a number of 'key issues' which it thought should be taken into account by any Bill. The Joffe Bill failed to adopt several. For example, the Committee recommended that consideration be given to a requirement that *any* applicant for PAS be given a psychiatric assessment, in order to confirm both that the request was based on a reasoned decision and free from external pressure, and that the applicant was not suffering from a psychiatric or psychological disorder causing impaired judgement. It added that where such disorder was apparent, it 'would expect an applicant to be offered treatment'. However, the Joffe Bill was more lax: it required referral only if there was doubt about an applicant's capacity, that is, if the patient might be 'unable to make a decision' about being assisted in suicide. It is hardly surprising that the Bill 'deeply worried' the Royal College of Psychiatrists.

Another Committee recommendation was that any Bill should consider requiring 'unrelievable' or 'intractable', rather than 'unbearable', suffering. However, the Joffe Bill persisted with 'unbearable suffering', which it defined as 'suffering, whether by reason of pain, distress or otherwise which the patient finds so severe as to be unacceptable'. In short, the criterion remained subjective.

A third recommendation was that any Bill should consider how patients seeking to end their lives might experience palliative care before taking a final decision. The Committee agreed with Lord Joffe that PAS 'should be considered only as a last resort' and thought it clear that something more than a simple consultation with a palliative care doctor or nurse was needed if patients contemplating PAS were to be able to make fully informed choices. If a Bill was to be able to claim with credibility that it was offering PAS as complementary with rather than as an alternative to palliative care, it might need to find a way of resolving this dilemma. By requiring only a simple consultation, the Joffe Bill failed to meet the Committee's concerns.

C. Extension and Abuse

As the Bill was essentially an alloy of the Oregon DWDA and the Dutch monitoring system, it was vulnerable to similar objections to those which have been levelled against the law in those two jurisdictions. In particular, the principles underlying the Bill called for its extension, and the Bill's 'safeguards' held out little prospect of preventing abuse.

i. Slippage in Principle

The Bill carried the seeds of its own extension from PAS to VAE and NVAE. Lord Joffe told the Committee (referring to his previous but broadly similar Bill) that the Bill was based on the principle of individual autonomy. But if personal autonomy was key, why its limitation to the terminally ill? He revealed that the limitation was due simply to the strength of political opposition and he added that he would support any move to extend the Bill to patients who were younger and not terminally ill but who were suffering unbearably. He also said he would prefer the Bill to be 'of much wider application' (a comment he withdrew during the second reading debate). 'Terminal illness' was not the only limit to conflict with autonomy. If autonomy was key, why permit PAS but not VAE? Why deny either PAS or VAE to those who wanted accelerated death and who were not suffering unbearably or even at all? Further, the Bill limited PAS to those who had attained the age of majority. Why, like the Dutch law, did it not respect the autonomous requests of legally competent patients under 18?

A further reason the Bill carried the seeds of its own extension is that a second principle underlay the Bill. Although Lord Joffe placed autonomy centre stage, the principle of beneficence was lurking in the wings. Lord Joffe admitted that the Bill was also based on the principle of 'humanity', and Lord Mackay pointed out that this principle applied both to the competent and to the incompetent. Why, then, did humanity/beneficence not require euthanasia for the incompetent? Further, how could beneficence justify the limitation of PAS to those whose suffering was 'unbearable', to those who had a 'terminal illness' and to those who were over 18?

Thirdly, it seems that, like several advocates of PAS/VAE (including Professor Jackson), Lord Joffe perceives little if any moral difference between PAS and other end-of-life decisions which shorten life. But if what matters morally to Lord Joffe is the shortening of life and not the doctor's intention, and if he accepts the shortening of the lives of patients, competent or incompetent, by withholding/withdrawing treatment, why did his Bill not permit the shortening of the lives of patients, competent or incompetent, by lethal injection? His testimony to the Committee disclosed no objection to NVAE in principle. He said, revealingly, there would perhaps need to be a different scheme for the incompetent because it could not rest on respect for autonomy.

In short, the Bill's broad limitations (to PAS, 'terminal illness', 'unbearable suffering' and adults) seem, as in Oregon, to have been little more than political expediency, concessions designed to entice the House of Lords to take the first step. Had that step been taken, those limitations would in time have buckled before the inexorable pressure of the very same principles, autonomy and beneficence, which had been invoked to justify that first step.

ii. Slippage in Practice

Lord Joffe claimed to the Committee that his Bill was considerably more restrictive and had more safeguards than the laws in Oregon and the Netherlands. In some respects he was right.

Unlike the Oregon law, his Bill required 'unbearable suffering' and, unlike the Dutch law, it did not permit VAE. In other respects, however, his Bill was less restrictive. The Oregon DWDA does not allow PAS for those suffering 'a psychiatric or psychological disorder, or depression causing impaired judgment'. Dutch law requires VAE/PAS to be a 'last resort', and that the doctor be interviewed by the local medical examiner. Even to the extent that the Bill contained further safeguards than the Oregon law on which it was modelled, those safeguards could not have ensured the protection of the vulnerable.

First, the Bill's most significant addition to the Oregon law, the incorporation of part of the Dutch monitoring system, hardly allayed concern. As we have seen,[165] that system has failed to prevent widespread breach of the law. Is there any reason to suppose that the Bill's system would have proved, as it has in the Netherlands, little more than a self-validating exercise by those doctors who choose to report? Secondly, the Bill, unlike the Oregon law, required the patient to be 'suffering unbearably', but this was a matter for the patient's subjective determination. Other supposed safeguards in the Bill, such as the requirement that the patient's declaration be witnessed by someone to whom the patient was known, or to whom the patient had proved his identity, were hardly reassuring. As Lord Carlile objected, there is a huge difference between someone being personally known to a witness and simply identifying them.

A hypothetical case will illustrate why any description of the Bill's safeguards as 'strict' would be misleading.

iii. 'Ethel'

Ethel is a lonely 85-year-old woman who has just been diagnosed with incurable breast cancer. Her GP has told her that her life expectancy without treatment is five months, and with treatment two years. Seriously depressed, she feels suicidal. She telephones

---

[165] See pp 124–28, 'The Netherlands'.

Roger, her cousin. Roger is her only surviving relative and sole beneficiary of her substantial estate. Roger encourages her to seek PAS. Ethel, who now feels lonelier and more despondent than ever, agrees. Roger turns to the *Yellow Pages*, finds a private clinic advertising 'assisted dying' and makes an appointment for her the following week.

At the clinic, Ethel sees Dr Adam, a GP, and tells him that she is 'suffering unbearably' from her illness. Dr Adam examines her briefly and reads the medical records that she has brought with her. He says that he has no reason to doubt what her records recount (that she is terminally ill and likely, without treatment, to die within six months) nor what she says (that she is suffering unbearably). He recommends PAS. Ethel mentions that her normal GP of many years has refused her request for PAS, but Dr Adam does not bother to contact him to find out why. Ethel then hands Dr Adam a letter, dictated by Roger and signed by herself, requesting PAS. Dr Adam gives her a leaflet describing the process of PAS under the 'Joffe Act' and alternatives to it. He calls in a clinic nurse who has undergone a short course in palliative care and who hands Ethel a leaflet about the benefits of palliative care. Dr Adam encourages Ethel to notify her next of kin (who is, of course, Roger). Ethel repeats that she wants PAS. The consultation, which has lasted 15 minutes, ends. Dr Adam then asks her to see another doctor at the clinic, Dr Black, an oncologist. Ethel sees Dr Black and repeats her request for PAS. Dr Black examines her and reads her medical records. He agrees with Dr Adam's diagnosis and prognosis, that she does not lack capacity and that she is suffering unbearably. He informs her of the alternatives to PAS. Ethel repeats her request for PAS, which Dr Black says he believes to be voluntary and informed. He tells her that prior to receiving her prescription for lethal drugs she will need to complete a declaration, which she can revoke if she wishes. After this second consultation, which has lasted 10 minutes, Dr Black suggests to Ethel that she might like to make her declaration at Smiths the nearby solicitors and to return for her lethal prescription in two weeks' time, together with a cheque for £10,000.

Neither Dr Adam nor Dr Black has any expertise in psychiatry. Both doctors fail to notice the symptoms of Ethel's disturbed mental state, symptoms which would have led a psychiatrist to conclude that she is so depressed as to be incompetent to request PAS. Ethel goes to Smiths who are solicitors to the clinic and who see many applicants for PAS referred by the clinic. She produces her driving licence as proof of identity and her declaration is witnessed by a young solicitor and his secretary. Unbeknown to Ethel the solicitor she sees, Tom, is a good friend of Roger's, and his secretary, Liz, is Roger's girlfriend. Two weeks later Ethel returns to the clinic. Dr Adam informs her of her right to revoke her declaration and asks whether she has done so. Ethel replies that she has not. Dr Adam gives her a prescription for lethal drugs. Back home Ethel informs Roger that she has obtained a lethal prescription. Eighteen months later, the doctors' prognosis of death within six months having proved inaccurate, Ethel's mental state has deteriorated so much that her incompetence would now be obvious even to a doctor without psychiatric expertise. Without the benefit of palliative care, she is also in acute, unrelieved pain. With Roger standing over her, and with his enthusiastic encouragement, she takes the lethal drugs. After several lingering hours, Ethel dies. Roger duly inherits Ethel's estate. Dr Adam has filed a report with the monitoring commission stating that the requirements of the Act were satisfied. Ethel's demise would have satisfied the Joffe Bill's 'safeguards'.

Enough has been said to show that such limitations as the Bill contained were little more than arbitrary lines in the sand, and that it would have exposed many vulnerable patients like Ethel to the real risk of making a request whose autonomy was flawed by pressure and/or depression. Rightly, the Bill was voted down by a substantial majority.

VI. CONCLUSIONS

The euthanasia debate is not new. Indeed, few questions have been the subject of so many expert inquiries. Those enquiries have, with rare exceptions, repeatedly rejected the case for VAE/ PAS (a fact which refutes the claim that opposition is essentially 'religious'). It is not difficult to see why that case has been repeatedly rejected. In section III we considered 10 arguments standardly advanced in favour of VAE/PAS, and found them far less cogent than they may superficially appear. Anyone concerned about the values of 'choice' and 'dignity' has (at least if those values are grounded in a sound understanding of human rights) every reason to defend rather than attack the present law. Moreover, given the impressive advances in palliative care in recent decades, the case for weakening the law has itself never been weaker.

The campaign for VAE/PAS trades on a few 'hard cases'. Every lawyer knows what hard cases make. As the Walton Committee concluded:

> We acknowledge that there are individual cases in which euthanasia may be seen by some to be appropriate. But individual cases cannot reasonably establish the foundation of a policy which would have such serious and widespread repercussions. Moreover dying is not only a personal or individual affair. The death of a person affects the lives of others, often in ways and to an extent which cannot be foreseen. We believe that the issue of euthanasia is one in which the interest of the individual cannot be separated from the interest of society as a whole.[166]

Assurances that society would be protected by 'safeguards' ring hollow. The Oregon safeguards are, as Professor Capron accurately described them, 'illusory'. Those in the Joffe Bill were scarcely better. Evidence produced by the Dutch themselves has shown that their guidelines have been widely flouted and with virtual impunity. The Dutch experience illustrates a key fact: *decriminalisation does nothing to reduce the opportunity for abuse*. Perhaps stricter safeguards would work? But if Dutch doctors have shown themselves unwilling to comply even with 'light touch' regulation, what is the prospect of physician compliance with

---

[166] Walton (n 2) para 237.

stricter regulation? The tighter the hand of regulation closes, the more cases are likely to slip through its fingers. There is an irreconcilable tension between medicalisation and regulation, between the inherently private, confidential nature of the doctor–patient interaction and subjecting it to external scrutiny and control.

The case for VAE/PAS is not only an invitation to deny the right to life which is grounded in the inherent and ineradicable dignity of all patients: it also contains the seeds of its own inexorable extension. If a doctor thinks that a patient who requests death would be 'better off dead', why deny that benefit merely because a patient cannot request it? The slippery slope from VAE/PAS to NVAE is not, then, merely a practical slope, reflecting the difficulty of framing and policing guidelines (though, as we have seen from the experience in the Netherlands and Oregon, that difficulty is real enough). It is a logical slope. If VAE/PAS are justified because some patients are 'better off dead', then so is NVAE. The current campaign for PAS is simply an attempt to get a foot in the door. It seeks to sell the illusion that PAS is centrally about patient autonomy. But once the smiling mask of autonomy is peeled away, we see the ugly face of euthanasia, marred by the belief that some members of our community would be 'better off dead'. The case for PAS may attract like the face of Dorian Gray, but its true portrait is hidden in the attic. If PAS is ethical, then so is euthanasia, both with and without request.

Emily Jackson openly endorses both. Rejecting the notion of inherent human dignity which grounds the Universal Declaration of Human Rights and the principle of the inviolability of human life, she holds that only certain human beings qualify as 'persons'. Only those of us who pass some arbitrarily selected and vaguely defined test (such as 'a mental life of a high order of sophistication') qualify. Those who do not are 'non-persons' or 'organisms' and may be treated like animals. The implications of this approach for the most vulnerable members of our community, such as those with dementia or severe learning disabilities, are chillingly clear. No wonder disability groups fervently oppose VAE/PAS.

Whenever society has denied basic rights to certain groups of human beings, whether on the basis of colour, religion, sex or disability, the results have been grim.

Professor Jackson's case is vulnerable not only because it distinguishes human beings from 'persons', but because it fails to distinguish between intending death and merely foreseeing death. This argument proves too little and too much. Too little in that it fails to dent the distinction, properly drawn by professional medical ethics, law and commonsense, between trying to kill the pain and trying to kill the patient, and between withdrawing a futile *treatment* and ending a 'futile' *life*. Too much in that it commits one to the untenable conclusions that doctors are performing non-voluntary euthanasia whenever they give palliative drugs to incompetent patients, foreseeing the drugs will shorten life, and involuntary euthanasia whenever they (because of, say, limited resources) withhold or withdraw a life-prolonging treatment from a patient who wants it. Professor Jackson's concern for the interests of patients is commendable, but those interests would be ill-served by VAE/PAS. Granting doctors the power to kill patients would give even more power to doctors (and society) and make patients, already in a vulnerable position, even more vulnerable. Tellingly, the law in the Netherlands and Oregon is drafted to protect doctors, not patients. Jackson claims 'safeguards' could prevent abuse but is very coy about telling us in any detail what they might look like. We have seen how 'safeguards' work, or rather don't, abroad and the undignified and unprotected way in which those in the Joffe Bill would have allowed a lady like Ethel to meet her end.

As the battery of expert bodies which have rejected the case for VAE/PAS have concluded, the way forward is not to weaken the protection afforded by the law, but to improve the quality and availability of palliative treatment for patients and of social support for patients and their carers. The Department of Health's End of Life Care Strategy, which was launched in 2008 and aims to ensure high-quality end-of-life care for everyone, is a welcome development. So too is the 2011 Palliative Care Funding Review.

It concludes that almost 100,000 people still lack access to good palliative care but that 'delivering improved recognition of palliative care needs, as well as optimised provision of services outside the hospital setting' could reduce deaths in hospital by 60,000 by 2021 and reduce hospital costs by £180 million per year.[167] The need for palliative care is even more acute in less developed countries, as Human Rights Watch has documented in its latest global audit.[168] A decade ago Ezekiel Emanuel wrote, as head of bioethics at the National Institutes of Health in the US, that it was time to turn away from the 'emotionally charged irrelevance' of the euthanasia debate and 'focus on the unglamorous process of systematic change to help the majority of dying patients'.[169] This should indeed be our urgent priority, from which the euthanasia debate is a tired and tiresome distraction. It is high time to euthanise the euthanasia debate.

What, then, is the 'take-home' message? First, either PAS, VAE and NVAE are (as Emily Jackson thinks) all ethical or (as I think) they are not. Secondly, they are wrong because they deny the inherent and ineliminable dignity we all share in virtue of our common humanity, a dignity which grounds our right not to be intentionally killed. Thirdly, weakening the law's historic defence of that right would discriminate against the most vulnerable in our community, not least the dying, the disabled and the disadvantaged.

---

[167] 'Funding the Right Care and Support for Everyone' (2011) 9. http://palliativecarefunding.org.uk/wp-content/uploads/2011/06/PCFRFinal%20Report.pdf.

[168] 'Global State of Pain Treatment' (2011) www.hrw.org/en/reports/2011/06/01/global-state-pain-treatment-0.

[169] EJ Emanuel, 'Euthanasia: Where the Netherlands Leads Will the World Follow?' (2001) 322 *British Medical Journal* 1376, 1377.

Bibliography

The euthanasia debate is vigorous and interdisciplinary and the literature it has generated is both vast and diverse. In this bibliography we point the reader to some of the significant and useful sources.

Books which contain philosophical contributions for and against are a good starting-point, including Gerald Dworkin, RG Frey and Sissela Bok (eds), *Euthanasia and Physician Assisted Suicide: For and Against* (Cambridge, Cambridge University Press, 1998), John Keown (ed), *Euthanasia Examined* (Cambridge, Cambridge University Press, 1995) and Dennis J Horan and David Mall (eds), *Death, Dying and Euthanasia* (Washington DC, University Publications of America, 1980).

Turning to philosophical works in favour of euthanasia, some, like James Rachels, *The End of Life: Euthanasia and Morality* (Oxford, Oxford University Press, 1986) and Robert Young, *Medically Assisted Death* (Cambridge, Cambridge University Press, 2007), focus on the end of life. Others address euthanasia as part of a broader analysis of the ethics of ending life. These include Jonathan Glover, *Causing Death and Saving Lives: The Moral Problems of Abortion, Infanticide, Suicide, Euthanasia, Capital Punishment, War and Other Life-or-Death Choices* (London, Penguin, 1990); Ronald Dworkin, *Life's Dominion: An Argument About Abortion, Euthanasia, and Individual Freedom* (New York, Alfred A Knopf, 1993); Peter Singer, *Rethinking Life and Death: The Collapse of Our Traditional Ethics* (Oxford, Oxford University Press, 1994) and Jeff McMahan, *The Ethics of Killing: Problems at the Margins of Life* (Oxford, Oxford University Press, 2002).

So it is with philosophical texts against. Some focus on euthanasia, such as German Grisez and Joseph M Boyle, *Life and Death with Liberty and Justice* (Notre Dame IN, University of Notre Dame

Press, 1979) and Luke Gormally (ed), *Euthanasia, Clinical Practice and the Law* (London, The Linacre Centre, 1994). Others range more widely, including John Finnis, *Human Rights & Common Good: Collected Essays Volume III* (Oxford, Oxford University Press, 2011); David S Oderberg, *Applied Ethics: a Non-consequentialist Approach* (Oxford, Wiley-Blackwell, 2000); Alfonso Gomez-Lobo, *Morality and the Human Goods: An Introduction to Natural Law Ethics* (Washington DC, Georgetown University Press, 2001) and Helen Watt, *Life and Death in Healthcare Ethics: A Short Introduction* (London, Routledge, 2000).

The legal literature on euthanasia is also voluminous. Lawyers have tended to focus less on philosophical arguments than on comparisons between the law in different jurisdictions, distinctions between euthanasia and other conduct which may or will shorten life, and the feasibility of drafting and enforcing legislation permitting euthanasia and/or physician-assisted suicide. Examples include Margaret Otlowski, *Voluntary Euthanasia and the Common Law* (Oxford, Oxford University Press, 2000); Penney Lewis, *Assisted Dying and Legal Change* (Oxford, Oxford University Press, 2007); Sheila McLean, *Assisted Dying: Reflections on the Need for Law Reform* (Abingdon, Routledge-Cavendish, 2007) and John Griffiths et al, *Euthanasia and Law in Europe* (Oxford, Hart Publishing, 2008), which support relaxation of the law, and Yale Kamisar, 'Some Non-Religious Views Against Proposed "Mercy-Killing" Legislation' (1958) 42 *Minnesota Law Review* 969 (reproduced in Horan and Mall, above); John Keown, *Euthanasia, Ethics and Public Policy* (Cambridge, Cambridge University Press, 2002) and Neil M Gorsuch, *The Future of Assisted Suicide and Euthanasia* (Princeton NJ, Princeton University Press, 2009), which oppose relaxation.

Contributions by medical authors occupy a significant place in the literature. Some favour relaxation of the law: see Raymond Tallis, 'Should the Law on Assisted Dying be Changed? Yes' (2011) 342 *British Medical Journal* d2355. Others do not: see Kathleen M Foley and Herbert Hendin (eds), *The Case against Assisted Suicide: For the Right to End-of-Life Care* (Baltimore MD, Johns Hopkins University Press, 2004)

Empirical research into the attitudes to and the practice of euthanasia is an important aspect of the debate. Sources include Roger Magnusson, *Angels of Death: Exploring the Euthanasia Underground* (New Haven CT, Yale University Press, 2002) and Clive Seale, 'End-of-Life Decisions in the UK Involving Medical Practitioners' (2009) 23 *Palliative Medicine* 198 and 'Legalisation of Euthanasia or Physician-Assisted Suicide: Survey of Doctors' Attitudes' (2009) 23 *Palliative Medicine* 205.

Finally, there have been many reports by expert bodies, both in the UK and beyond. An important report in the US is that of the New York State Task Force on Life and the Law, *When Death is Sought: Assisted Suicide and Euthanasia in the Medical Context* (1994). The reports of two House of Lords Select Committees, their volumes of evidence, and the debates in the House of Lords upon those reports are a mine of information and argument. Much of this material is accessible online. The first Select Committee, chaired by Lord Walton, reported in 1994 (*Report of the Select Committee on Medical Ethics* (HL 1993–94, 21-I)). The second, chaired by Lord Mackay, reported in 2005 (*Report of the Select Committee on the Assisted Dying for the Terminally Ill Bill* (HL 2004–05, 86-I)). A more recent report is that of a Committee appointed by the Scottish Parliament: *End of Life Assistance (Scotland) Bill Committee Report* (SP Paper 523) www.scottish.parliament.uk/s3/committees/ endLifeAsstBill/reports-10/ela10-01-vol1.htm. Another relevant official publication is the UK Department of Health's *End of Life Care Strategy* (2008) www.dh.gov.uk/en/Publicationsandstatistics/ Publications/PublicationsPolicyAndGuidance/ DH_086277 and a related publication is Rachael Addicott and Rebecca Ashton (eds), *Delivering Better Care at End of Life* (London, The King's Fund, 2010).

Some useful websites are:

Patients Rights Council (US): www.patientsrightscouncil.org/site. Carenotkilling Alliance (UK): www.carenotkilling.org.uk/.

Dignity in Dying (UK): www.dignityindying.org.uk/.
Compassion and Choices (US): www.compassionandchoices.org.

Index